Diving to extreme skiing
chapter 8 memory

The Conscious Sale

Using the power of state, intention and belief:

A guide to sales success

Taran Hughes

Print edition

Acknowledgements

I would like to thank my family and friends for their encouragement and support through the process of writing this book, and of course a big thank you to Wilson for all his wisdom and teaching.

CONTENTS

Preface

I once read a book that told me to start with why, so I am going to start with my why. Why it is I have written this book. I have been in sales for over 20 years, 15 of which have been in telecoms, and the last six of those in sales management. During this time I have worked with many clients and salespeople. Over the years I've made many cold calls, written countless proposals, attended a lot of meetings, and to be fair, closed a large share of deals, but it has only been during the last six years that I have started to understand what really causes "success", and therefore what makes people successful.

In July 2014, I left my role as sales director with a large telecoms company and, unaware as I was at that time, it was to be the start of my journey. My departure to some, to many in fact, could have easily been looked upon as the end of something rather than the beginning. However I was excited, excited at the prospect of the unknown, which was odd, principally because prior to that point I had not considered a change. I was relatively happy; I had built a good team around me, believed in the ability of the company, and felt we were contributing to our clients' needs in a meaningful way. That said, I had felt for some time that there was something missing, something else with a purpose I could be doing.

So in early July I had agreed my exit. I decided to spend some time overseas and travelled throughout parts of Southeast Asia, together with some other places I had wanted to visit. I returned to the UK towards the end of the year, having had a great time and met many interesting people but for all the time spent away I wasn't any clearer on what I might do next. In January 2015, through a chance encounter I was introduced to an entrepreneurial business group. Unlike other groups I had encountered, at the heart of this group sat the principles of mindfulness and awareness of the self, and how that awareness impacts what you experience in your business life.

I realised what I had previously felt, that feeling of something missing, was the desire to create something for myself. I had been part of the group for several months but wasn't feeling inspired by any of the businesses I had encountered, nor did I have a clear idea of what I might do. Then in May, some four months later, I had an idea, and that idea was to write this material. You see it dawned on me that the principles and behaviours that so commonly underpin successful entrepreneurs, those same values that the group I belonged to held great stock in, were entirely appropriate or even needed in the wider sales environment.

What my tenure in the telecoms industry had shown me was that there existed a real gap between the expectations of clients and the intentions of the sales force that served them, and that gap became increasingly more apparent the larger the organisation became. It also became evident that salespeople can be their very own worst enemy, with unconscious self-sabotage of situations and opportunities only contributing further to the observed gap.

With the perspective of time and some distance from the situations I myself had been involved in, I came to see that there were three sets of needs from three sets of participants, the client, the sales rep and the supplier organisation. I will set my focus upon the sales rep and client for the purpose of this material, as I feel the desires and objectives of organisations to be evident to those that work within them. Within that dynamic there were several misaligned goals, at least for the rep and supplier; as with most large organisations there was a continued move to extract more from less, that's to say find productivity efficiencies through a streamlined workforce, and that premise is also in part what has shaped many organisations the world over. So much so that the salesman and the telecoms buyer of today have come a long way from their counterpart of 10 years ago.

The pursuit of efficiency is felt throughout the entire corporate structure; today's employee across all departments is increasingly being burdened with more responsibilities as manpower resources are reduced. The net consequence of this means time is becoming an ever scarcer resource, and consequently, meaningful relationships between the supplier and buyer may not develop as freely as they might once have, especially if the time spent with clients is looked upon as a means to an end rather than the focus for that particular point in time.

What I am saying is that it's increasingly common amongst salespeople to chase something in the future, a deal, a number or even just recognition, rather than being focused or mindful of what they are engaged in in the present moment. When that happens there is disconnect, because the objectives of each party aren't aligned and will ultimately diverge. The salesperson is looking for a number and the associated commission, whereas the buyer is looking for a solution to a business need.

The irony in all of this is that the salesperson who is driven by the attainment of a future goal is missing the point, primarily because the future outcome can only be affected by actions and awareness of what is happening in the present moment. Whereas if the prevailing focus and awareness of why you are sitting opposite your client is how you can better serve them in that moment, and an attendant idea to this is to question what value can you bring, then there is an alignment of interests between the two parties and when that happens the buyer's primary needs can be met and consequently the salesperson's goal, the sale and associated commission, becomes possible as a byproduct of the process.

It is my intention to introduce through this material a deeper dimension of awareness to the sales process within businesses large and small, one that complements proven sales methodologies commonly practised. By studying the principles of awareness contained, and by adopting the principles articulated within each, you can experience more flow and consistency in each aspect of your role and be empowered to excel in your duty to your clients. You can do this by delivering disproportionate value through awareness of your own state, intentions and beliefs. The alignment of the three principles, applied to the deep knowledge of your marketplace, together with continuous evaluation and qualification, of yourself and how you serve your client, will result in greater consistency within your sales performance and stronger client relationships.

As with any discipline, this must be practised daily, but to the sceptical voice within you I encourage you not to take what I say on face value; rather try the approach for yourself and be the proof you would seek. Although this material is concerned with the specifics of sales engagement, the positives are not constrained here. It is my belief that through the adoption of these principles it is indeed likely you will notice a positive change permeating throughout other areas of your life.

Part 1 – The Conscious Sale

Chapter 1 – Success is an Inside Job

Before you read any further, I want you to take a moment to ask yourself: Why are you reading this book?

Whatever has brought this material to you, in order for you to get the full benefit from it I make a small request: simply that for the duration of this material, you make a commitment to reading with an open mind. That may sound simple enough, but go ahead, say it out loud and mean it. Furthermore, as part of that commitment, can you resist the use of three little words whilst reading this book? They are words that we have most likely uttered out loud or under our breath at one time or another. The words? “I know that!”

Coming from a background in telecoms sales, I have worked with a lot of smart, experienced sales guys, and over the years I have noticed that in varying situations their ego would be expressed strongly. This was most noticeable during sales meetings where their accounts and activity were put under the microscope, measuring their level of understanding towards the account opportunity being worked on. Often an undercurrent of “Why are you asking me, I know that?” would be in the background of their response, and for the most part they did know their accounts and opportunities. However in a learning environment it’s important to set aside that part of yourself, that part that knows it all, the ego; after all that’s what it is.

The truth is our ego doesn’t like admitting to anything that diminishes itself, that’s to say admitting something that might have been missed or to anything that makes it feel smaller. This is often an unconscious occurrence. If you are sitting there and saying to yourself, “What is he talking about, I don’t have an ego, or if I do it is in check”, well, that voice in your head, the one that speaks to you when referring to the self without prompting, often never being quiet for long, that’s the voice of the ego.

So with this in mind, can I ask you to make a conscious decision to be open to learning from this material? If it helps pay some mind to something Albert Einstein once said: "The more I learn, the more I realize how much I don't know." The truth is in sales we only know what we know, and until we accept that we don't know everything we cannot become aware of what we need to know, and if you are not aware of that, you cannot learn something new; it is just not in your awareness.

If you can let go of the egoic voice in your head for the duration of this book, the one saying that you know this stuff already, then your awareness can be broadened and you will certainly permit yourself a new perspective on what actually influences sales situations and the people involved. From this place you will see how it is possible to improve the results you get from the 86,400 seconds of your day.

You may well have already undertaken sales training courses in the past, so it's likely you're aware that the main principles of successful selling have been accurately and comprehensively stated by numerous authors and methodologies. Nonetheless even with the best sales strategies followed to the tee, why is it that some people just seem to have better luck when it comes to building relationships and hitting targets?

Firstly then let us start with what we all know, that first and foremost consistently successful salespeople always have a strong pipeline and awareness of the correlation between success and pipeline values. The more qualified opportunities in your sales funnel you have the more confident you are in achieving your number; that is a simple fact. At one time or another we have all sat in a sales pipeline review and either squirmed under questioning in the knowledge that we had a weak sales funnel or conversely sat there with a conviction that the sales number was secured. Not just because of the deal or deals you expected to close but due to the fact that you had plenty of capacity in upside opportunity, and that your confidence came from a feeling of abundance.

Obvious really! You cannot close what you do not have, which is why there is always huge emphasis placed on focused attention towards prospecting for new opportunities, whether that's from within your base or new, yet to be contacted potential clients.

When you only have two opportunities to work on to make your number you have a heightened sense of pressure to close them both. Perhaps your interpretation of every detail or occurrence becomes critical: the fact that the client is not picking up the phone today becomes far more ominous, placing greater pressure on the outcome. Whereas given another time, with more opportunities to draw from to make the number, you might otherwise put it down to them being busy and you will be confident that you will reach them the next time you call.

With a heightened sense of pressure the mind starts to conjure all manner of unattractive possible reasons for what might be happening. Maybe you feel you are not close enough to the deal, or perhaps your offering is not priced keenly enough. That sense of pressure must affect the way you feel about the deal's likelihood of closing and in turn influence the way you respond to and proceed with progressing the sale and the necessary steps within the sales cycle to a point of closing.

In that situation, is it confidence that shines through to the client or is there a whiff of desperation, even if it is not in the spoken sense, what about energetically? Maybe you are calling them a little more frequently, perhaps pushing in the meeting a little more than normal. Are you even aware of it? Does it change the way you interact with your peers, your manager? The stressed-out sales guy under pressure within the team was easily spotted; it might have been subtle but the tells were always there. It would change their demeanour and behaviour with those around them. Everything was a little more serious, their tolerance of disappointment that little less abundant, and their sense of urgency a little more prevalent.

Is that scenario something you can relate to? In truth I think all salespeople experience it to varying degrees at times throughout their careers. If you don't notice it in yourself maybe it is easier to spot in your colleagues as we often see things more clearly in others. Energetically what is going on here points to a principle that many describe as abundance vs. scarcity. The opposite of the scarcity described above is being abundant. "I have plenty of opportunity; I will hit my number!" That feeling does not change or alter the reality that the deal still has to be closed, however there exists a real confidence based on an abundance of opportunities from which to make the sales quota. That said, what is that confidence really, other than a strong sense of belief or knowing? In the awareness stakes there are three states we operate from, and each has in relative terms a value.

Firstly we form a thought around something – "I think I can..." It translates to a supposition that the desired outcome is possible, as in the closing of a deal, but also recognising that it might not close – with the weighting of the doubt being at least equal to the notion of possibility.

Then there is the second state of awareness, the belief in the expected or desired outcome.

Energetically this is much stronger than a thought you might hold about something. The bias of belief about something is that of predominant success in whatever the endeavour is, but there does remain an element of doubt as to the outcome, albeit a small one.

Finally there is knowing, a resolute awareness of the outcome being that which you determine. You know it like you know it like you know it. There is no element of uncertainty or doubt entertained. It's a given just like gravity.

With that being said, the truth is that they are still only feelings experienced, and until the contract is actually signed they are just the feeling we might have about the situation, but they alter dramatically the energy with which we approach activities and the way we are received by those around us.

We can all relate to each of these scenarios if we explore our own experiences. For example, "I think I will hit my quota next month" really says something like "I don't know if I am going to make my number". We don't actually say this because our ego will not allow us to be in such a vulnerable position, one where we might lose face, look like we aren't in control or less able than we wish to be seen as. In the sales meeting or when questioned by our management we use language that reflects our underlying feelings towards the deal. A diluted confidence is reflected in less certain sentiment and language: "I think" rather than "I know".

Then there is "I believe" as in "I believe I can smash my quarter number", which translates to "I am doing well", perhaps with some solid wins so far and enough business that it is possible to see it being a huge quarter. There is much stronger energy behind the statement and the feeling of belief is tangible, resolved to certain deals and elements such as verbal promises, alignment of clients' buying criteria and a strong match on the needs and solution, but there still remains a small but real sense that a risk remains, albeit calculated and quantified.

Finally there is knowing: "I know the deal will close this month because I have built a solid relationship with the decision maker and am aware of the sign-off process in detail. We have a really strong value proposition addressing their needs, and we have been told the business is ours and we are discussing terms." The energy behind this will allow you to stand up and state out loud the strength of your convictions – your confidence is high and you are not entertaining any doubt about the outcome. This is not to be confused with arrogance, which is a reflection of pride, often denying potential risks, and will most certainly catch you out sooner or later.

The person that "knows" is aware of the landscape they operate within. They remain pragmatic about what needs to be covered but have the underlying knowing that their solution and relationship is ultimately the best match. That best match is the outcome of the time invested with the client understanding their needs, and winning the hearts and minds of the wider buying team with a consistent approach to identifying issues and working together to find the resolution.

Yet all that has been stated is simply a reflection of how the individual feels about their opportunities and situations. The difference between the three states described is an inner condition, how we might be feeling about a set of external circumstances related to a sales opportunity. If that is the case, does it follow that the inner feeling is the reflection of what is happening on the outside, in the world at large, or is the outer experience of being in prime position for a stellar quarter a reflection of an inner state? More simply put, do we see the world as it is or do we see the world as we are? Am I successful because I observe successful outcomes to my actions or do I experience successful outcomes because they reflect my inner belief of what success is? Now that's a big question, one that we will explore further.

What is it that so-described "successful people" do that is so different to the majority? Whilst we are at it, what is meant by success anyway? It is not something that can be held in your hand. It is not tangible in that sense. In trying to quantify it we are actually measuring something else, typically the measure of our progress or achievement against a goal or objective, and in doing so we derive our sense of what success means from that achievement.

So if success cannot be tangibly measured in its own right because it is a feeling, a sense derived from something else, why do two seemingly similar people have varying experiences and results? Why does one salesperson experience more success than the other if the reality of success is only a feeling; why don't we all feel more successful? Perhaps it is down to something as simple as the two salespeople in question having differing thoughts towards what success is. What if success to the high achiever is not a measure of the personal win in the traditional sense that many subscribe to, but rather a win for the client they serve and the successful accomplishment of each aspect of what they do? Furthermore, perhaps the experience of success is cumulative, a consequential experience of consistently doing the simple things, ordinary things, extraordinarily well?

In each of the sales and management positions I have held over the years there was a common recurring sentiment prevalent throughout the sales environment. If you make your number each month, each quarter, every year, you will be successful in this company!

Have you ever considered what success actually is? Because if you think about it success is intangible; it is not something you can actually quantify. Are you successful when someone tells you that you are a success? "Well done, you made your quarter; you are successful"; so sayeth the manager. Is it at that point you feel a success?

Despite what people think and many might suggest, counting myself within that group for a huge part of my career, a success is not something that you can become. In the external world it might appear that you or someone you observe may encounter what we commonly describe as success. Logically you might reason that during some measured period of time that they or another became successful, but this seems to be a misperception. The mistake to this is thinking that the external perception of success precedes the inner experience or feeling.

Logically you might reason that during some measured time period, your month, your quarter, your year, you became successful, but if we examine the work that takes place during those time periods we can see that it is not true. Did you become successful on a single day?

Success is not tangible; it's a feeling, an experience brought about as a measure of something we accomplish. If it is experiential then by that rationale it can only be experienced in the now. So in the sense that you wish to experience success, it is something that you can only *be*: you can only be successful in the present moment.

If we encounter success as an inward experience first, why then is it that business as a whole commonly defines success as something outward, in the future, to be attained? "Hit your quarter and you will be successful! Do this and you will get the promotion; do that and receive the bonus!" Is it because we have blended together the meeting of certain contractual goals and objectives with our sense of success? The expectations of the companies we work for are totally legitimate: we are being paid to promote and sell the products and services of our firm, and in return for meeting those performance targets we receive our rewards such as sales commissions and promotions. However, within that transaction we have entwined the experience of success and more restrictively we have accepted as the norm the experience of success being only achievable as a consequence of the accomplishment of a narrow band of circumstances. We simply do not see success as something that we are being in what we are doing, as in successful in the present moment, in the activity we are engaged in. We accept the experience of success as being consequential rather than experiential.

In the sense that salespeople wish to experience success, it is something that you can only be; you can only be successful. That is to say, you can only be successful in the present moment. Commonly salespeople define success as something outward, that they attain through the meeting of certain goals or objectives such as sales awards and commissions. How often is success perceived as something that you are being in what you are doing, that is to say successful in the present moment, in the activity you are engaged in?

How aware are you of the success in the varying aspects of what you are doing? Whether it's listening to a client's needs or situational challenges, whether it's writing the notes up from the meeting, or maybe presenting, anything that you are doing in the present moment; be successful in that moment. That means ensuring there is a *sense of quality* in that activity, task or job. A purity gained through single-mindedness, clear awareness of what you are engaged in in that precise moment. In doing so you will start to become successful in each and every endeavour whilst your focus is taken up with the activity in that moment.

This means there is a sense of quality flowing into the activity, task or job. The more successful you are in the little things the more likely you are to attract successful outcomes in the larger things that you do. It is not surprising then that the practice of focused attention to each and every thing you undertake has an accumulating effect. That the feeling of accomplishment will continue to grow within you, and the practice will add greater depth to your confidence to undertake and excel in ever greater challenges. From that place a sense of enjoyment, which can be described as flow, starts to develop.

Therefore success in the little things begets greater success. If we break this down into logical steps, the success of closing a deal is divided into various stages of the sales cycle. It follows that for each one of those stages you must be successful to progress to the next. It is not as if you ever walked into your client's office one morning, slapped a contract down on their desk, thrust a pen in their hand and said "Sign it". The process must be observed and progressed through. Very simply put, you must successfully complete all stages in the sales cycle. The qualifying meeting, followed by successfully building and pricing a solution, successfully composing a proposal, the successful delivery of your presentation – all that must happen and be signed off internally before you can even start to consider talk of contracts. These are the gross aspects of the sales process; the finer, smaller, details are the listening aspects when meeting the client. The attention that you place on each and every component of that process that makes up the milestone in the sales cycle.

Those little successes that are internal to you do not require any recognition, any pats on the back, whether it be from your peers, the customer or your manager. Each success is simply building upon the last, growing larger, silently, without ego. This actually speaks louder than if you made a big deal of it. The irony now is that the success you started off thinking that you wanted, namely money, adulation, or recognition, actually starts to become a secondary goal. The primary goal, that is, your primary success, is now found in each moment, in each activity, culminating in the final close of the business. That is the success of knowing your performance has contained within it a quality. A quality imbued into every aspect of the work you have undertaken. You have done everything with a sense of focus, clarity and purpose which you may not normally direct into all your tasks, workflows and opportunities.

You will recognise this, sensing when you have done a good piece of work: there will be a feeling of quality that has been invested into the task. Although it does not mean that you give a little fist pump and say "Yeah! Look what I've done", you just have an inner knowing that you have put meaning into that piece of work because you can, because you wanted to, because you are building on something larger than for recognition; and in that moment when you're working in that capacity you are without ego, being in true service to your client. That is authenticity, and that is powerful in building successful relationships. All of your psychic or mental energy, the entirety of your focus, can be directed to the sole purpose of completing to the best and highest of your ability the task at hand.

The energy directed in this manner is considerably more than you may normally have available because at some level the energy and focus available to you on a day-to-day basis is consumed in varying degrees by the ego, by being self-conscious, concerned with how you are being seen, what others might think of you and of your work. When you are able to let go of that, and that is only really achievable when you fully occupy your attention with what you are doing, then to those around you, your peers, clients, managers etc, the silent quality in your work becomes highly visible.

It is time to stop listening to an insane world, one telling you what success is and from which you have measured so much of your achievement in the past. No longer let it tell you that success is something to be gained in the future. You can be successful right now simply by focusing your attention and ability on what you are engaged with in the present moment. That is why I say success is an inside job. Your power to consistently experience it in your work is greatly influenced by the energetic *state* you maintain, the *intentions* you set and the strength of your *belief* in them. How these are to be employed by you is what I have laid out in the following chapters.

Chapter Summary

Success is an Inside Job

- Make a conscious commitment to learning.
- Let go of what you think you already know.
- Start to see being successful as something to experience in the now, in the present moment, not as a future goal.
- The present moment is the only place and time you can experience success because only in the present moment can you take action.

Chapter 2 – The Marketplace Dynamic

The sales industry and the way that we transact with our clients is changing; there is no escaping the impact of technological innovation on the way that companies are enabling their clients to purchase. The pace at which it continues to change is accelerating as technology continues to facilitate the simplification of the buying experience. Whether one chooses to label this as "good" or "bad" is not the focus here and is entirely for you to decide. That said, some argue that if technological progress makes life simpler then it has a beneficial effect.

What if, however, the increase in the rate of this change is down to your clients' desire to experience something different to the hitherto conventional sales engagement, rather than the rate of innovation and the financial motives of the services provider? Throughout today's sales landscape it is no longer acceptable to simply visit a client, tell them about your products or services, then ask what keeps them awake at night and hope they have time to do your job for you. It might have been a sound approach once but it no longer serves the client or the sales rep.

In fact, the client "buying landscape" has changed dramatically, or more accurately stated, the way in which clients make buying decisions has changed. So much so that, according to a study conducted by Corporate Executive Board (CEB), of more than 1500 customer contacts for 23 large US B2B customers across varied industries, it was revealed that over 55% of typical purchase decisions are actually being made before the client even talks with a supplier.[1]

Over half your customers are only calling you in to validate the decision they have already made, or put bluntly, one in every two

---

[1] CEB – The Digital Evolution in B2B Marketing, p.2.
https://www.cebglobal.com/marketing-communications/digital-evolution.html

sales opportunities that you participate in, in your clients' eyes, you're there only to validate an already made decision and not affect one. That is a large percentage, and even if we accept this as being representative of all transaction types, ranging from the simple through to the complex sale, it is still a sobering thought.

A further glimpse of a possible reality to come for the salesperson is that by 2020, according to Forrester, it is forecast that one million salespeople will have lost their jobs to be replaced by automated, self-service e-commerce solutions in the US alone.[2] That figure represents more than 20% of the business-to-business sales force in America today.

So the question must be asked, what is driving businesses, that is to say people, to prefer dealing with a website rather than another human being?

It's not an unreasonable question to pose, since most people prefer to deal with live people either face to face or at the end of the telephone. I can recall numerous times of frustration when dealing with service providers via a helpline and being forced to deal with an automated service, or worse, with web-based support where it isn't entirely clear if you are dealing with a real person or some very smart software, something increasingly common as technology advancements continue to gain pace in the world of AI.

According to a prediction made at their customer 360 Summit back in 2011 Gartner, a leading American information technology research and advisory firm, predict that by 2020 85% of the relationships between enterprise and customer will be managed without any human interaction.[3] With consumer demand for unique and positive experiences, businesses will have to implement smart technologies to keep up. With that in mind it would seem that the corporate service provider is just following a path that has been laid

---

[2] https://www.forrester.com/report/Death+Of+A+B2B+Salesman/-/E-RES122288

[3] Gartner.com Gartner Customer 360 Summit 2011.

out, pioneered by the big B2C service providers such as banks, utility companies, phone and broadband suppliers. That well-trodden path, with the right implementation, will be a means to reduce the cost of sales and simplify the placement and taking of customer orders, something most companies strive to do.

So we can see what is in it for the corporate services providers and manufacturers: less costs, fewer salaries, a reduction in commissions paid, and the advantages of a standardised portfolio of services. With an online portal no longer will it be possible for services to be sold that fall outside the standard offering – frequently the cause of delivery teams and project managers' complaints about salespeople. Therefore, we can see the advantages for the service provider, but why are our clients willing to embrace online and e-commerce ordering for their business solutions?

Surely germane to the client is the idea that their needs must be accurately understood to ensure the perceived benefits of the service being procured are actually realised, which they hope translates into increased bottom line, operational advantage or competitive edge. So why the computer, and not meaningful communications with a real person? A salesperson that takes into consideration all of the relevant aspects of their client's organisation, who is then able to tailor a solution specific to the client's needs rather than adopt a one-size-fits-all approach delivered through a web portal?

And maybe the answer is being pointed towards by the words "meaningful communications". Maybe what has been lost in the sales experience, in the pursuit of corporate efficiencies and greater market share, what clients are craving, is simply a much better customer experience with meaningful communications. Those that fulfil their expectations of service and value, with salespeople focused upon the understanding of their client needs, their marketplace and delivery on what has been promised. After all, if experience proves to the buyer time after time that it is the human element which reduces the customer experience to such a poor level, then it's not so hard to see why many buyers will choose to order through an online system.

This shift in behaviour is further supported by the statistical evidence that over 50% of buyers have already made the decision on what to buy before even engaging the salesperson. This reflects significant changes to their buying approach: if the need for an interactive relationship with a salesperson continues to diminish then it becomes a small step to an environment predominantly serving businesses online and it charts the change from an interactive consultative sale to a transactional one. So then, if we are to pay credence to the statistical data available, why is it that salespeople across many industries are failing to deliver on what their organisation promises, and more importantly what the client expects? Are we not operating in a culture of supply and demand? Is that not the basis on which organisations operate, supplying what their clients want?

If the salesperson misses the underlying desire of their client to receive a consistent quality sales experience, one that creates innovative solutions rather than reducing them to a number against a sales target, then we really don't need to look too far to understand how we got to where we are or where we are heading.

What is the alternative narrative? What happens when we get things right for those business relationships where the right focus and mindset is applied? Well, it is reflected back to the salesperson and the company, going beyond just the securing of the contract or order. There opens up the possibility of a much closer working relationship, because the relationship was founded on respect and understanding of the client and their needs, rather than of the interests of the salesperson. What typically becomes clear to the client is the authenticity of the salesperson acting on their behalf as an agent of possibility: someone that places the client at the fore of their awareness and works towards their goals as if they too were employed by the client company. Over time this builds trust, which becomes loyalty, and that can be a great measure of the success we seek to experience.

Perhaps this is what distinguishes mediocrity from brilliance amongst sales professionals: that it is the way they choose to

approach their profession together with the attitu towards themselves and their clients that sets them apa

Now let us get some perspective on what the split between the customer-centric salespeople and those that fall short looks like. Whilst not identical in the numbers I cannot help but recall the old axiom of 80% of the business being generated by 20% of the sales force. If Pareto's Law when applied to business is correct, what is it then that the 20% do differently? If we can truly discern the differences, should it then be possible to apply those principles to bring about great improvement?

You see, what I have believed for some time, and others are starting to discover for themselves, is that what actually makes that small percentage of sales professionals so "successful", that is to say consistent in their sales achievement and commonly highly respected and trusted by their clients, is far less activity driven and more mindset focused.

For many, but certainly not all, it may be surprising to learn that the success we speak of, and I mean by that the successful building of relationships, those that meet the expectations of both the client business and the salesperson's own organisation, that success is far less about finding compelling reasons, matching terms and competitive pricing. It is not about that; those aspects of the sales process are a given and must be present in the deal. What is more noticeable about these successful individuals is their mindset and awareness towards their clients. It is the awareness of themselves, that they are sales professionals, and how they meet every situation within the continuing sales engagement process of which they are part. I have come to view this awareness and behavioural change as a paradigm shift, being represented by specific areas. To make this communicable I have structured these aspects into three areas, termed as the three Points of Conscious Performance. Each point interlaces with the others, and has been arrived at through the examination of my own experience within the world of sales and sales management.

To help convey some of the ideas and mechanics of what is placed in front of you we will refer to sports and business success to assist in illustrating some of the points in action. We will also draw from the world of scientific research to illuminate some of the darkness around why the mind does what it does when left to its own devices. This material is a journey and if followed it is intended to challenge you. I do not wish you to blindly accept what is written; go inside yourself every time something is difficult to hear or incongruent with your thoughts about it. If or rather when that happens it is suggested that you ask yourself why. Why is there resistance? Be honest with yourself and keep asking yourself this question to find the root cause of the resistance.

It may well be that you are unable to resolve all of the challenges that arise, but it is only your decision to examine and integrate the ideas into your practices that will ultimately validate the ideas I offer. Otherwise you are the coach standing on the edge of the playing field failing to call out the shots, never knowing if your game plays will bring the results you want.

The closer examination of your thoughts and feelings about the subject matter will bring you closer to the truth of why you are who you are as a salesperson and allow you to see how your thoughts and emotions play out, unconsciously shaping the texture of your interpretation of the events as they unfold around you. Those events, when dispassionately looked upon, can be broken down and viewed through the lens of one or more of the three Points of Conscious Performance.

With all this being said, to be effective as a sales professional you must also know your subject matter. Immersion in the products or services, including those of your customers, is key. Your awareness of the issues and trends of the day for your client's industry is now more important than ever; this is far easier if you are working within a specific market vertical or if you sell into a niche market. We see this more with large organisations recognising the value of industry verticalisation within sales in order to rationalise sales messaging such that it's much closer aligned to their specific target client.

Experience has reflected that the buyer of today is a far cry from the one being sold to 15 years ago, as companies operate with leaner infrastructure with less people now carrying greater responsibility. This translates to sweating resources in order to maximise efficiency and profitability; the customer of today is a lot more market savvy than his counterpart of yesterday. They know a lot about the offerings in the market, and are acutely aware of what keeps them awake at night.

Strong relationships get built over time; energy must be invested to bring about a seed change in the quality of business between each party together with the rewards they can deliver. For those of you seeking a change to the way your business relationships begin and develop over time, the following chapter will place before you structural questions about your motivations as a sales professional, exploring if what were true of your motives yesterday remains the same today, together with accounts of my own experience that played a hand in the direction my career took.

Chapter Summary

The Marketplace Dynamic

- Aim to add value to client meetings and interactions by being a subject matter expert in your area.
- Successful relationships require investment of energy and focus, so understand what your client needs and help them achieve that goal.
- Adopting a success mindset is a consistent factor in successful sales professionals.

Chapter 3 – How to be in Service to Your Clients

Service as a journey

We might easily look upon a sales opportunity as a journey taken with our clients. Considered this way, for the salesperson the journey's end, the desired "signed contract", is a long way off from the starting position of that first phone call or meeting. We travel down a road pausing at various stages, each marking progress through the sale, each of which must be navigated successfully before progressing to the next. It follows then, if the sales process is a journey travelled along with the client, that like any journey there must be a destination, but is the destination you choose the same as your client's? The idea that the destination of your sales journey is to "make the company money through signing a contract" may be a given even if it's not consciously set; it's tacitly implied that as a sales professional you are working to that end in all and every commercial engagement undertaken.

But two questions arise you may do well to ask yourself. Firstly, do you and your client have the same destination in mind? Is your win really the same as your client's? Secondly, from a broader perspective, how many of the tasks and activities associated with the opportunities you are engaged in do you actually set a plan for in order to reach that desired destination? We will look in much detail at the importance of setting plans, or rather setting intentions, later in the book. For now we will explore the first question as to the coincidence of destination between you and your client. If the research carried out points to anything then it is that a great many salespeople are failing to deliver the sales experience their clients are looking for. Maybe in order to answer the question of coincidence of destination we need to understand where we are coming from as salespeople.

To uncover that it may be useful to understand why you chose a career in sales. If you can't immediately answer the why question then perhaps it is easier to answer the question of how. Did you make a "conscious decision" or did you just end up in sales? Judging by the results of the Forrester analysis[4] reflecting only 11% of executive buyers being satisfied with the sales engagement of their supplier sales representatives, it would seem that a great many salespeople have lost their way in terms of their why. Why else would there be such a disparity between what buyers want and what they receive? With careers taking up such a large part of our lives, how is it that so many might be getting it so wrong with their clients, or worse, not actually enjoying what they do? Within this chapter I want to look at how we as individuals and collectively as a profession can get back on track and close the gap and develop meaningful relationships with our clients.

So let us start with your WHY? It's a good question to ask from time to time, especially as we get all too easily caught up with the often-frantic continuous stream of demands on our time and attention such that we rarely take a moment to reflect, not on what we are doing, but the WHY behind it. So take a moment to ask yourself, why are you a salesperson? Explore the question and see if you can get in touch with the ideas and thinking that led you down the path of a professional sales career. What was it that attracted you to sales? Take some time and jot down your thoughts, feelings and ideas on the matter to help you. Just considering this question will allow for your awareness to examine if the values and ideas that set you on this path are still congruent with who you are today, or whether you have over time just reduced those ideas and beliefs to the simple and commonplace position that you do what you do to maintain your place in society, to make a living, meeting financial and social demands placed upon you by yourself and the society you play a part in. There is of course nothing wrong with that, but the relationship between what you do and the results you experience are connected. If the undertaking of any activity is simply going through the motions, a means to getting somewhere without really engaging with the work as it unfolds, then the output, whether internal, such as

[4] https://www.forrester.com/report/Death+Of+A+B2B+Salesman/-/E-RES122288

your sense of fulfilment, or external, such as the res experience, will lack depth and meaning.

I didn't actually wake up one day and decide that I wanted a career in sales; it was far more accidental but nonetheless the seed was sown in my mind at a young age. My father was an entrepreneur and over the years ran several different businesses. I guess my love of business was greatly influenced by him. My first experience in sales was when I was 14 years old. At that time my parents owned several shops including a delicatessen. Quite often there would be unsold bread and I quickly saw an opportunity to make sandwiches and rolls from the day-old bread and leftover cold cuts, selling them to the other kids at school. This turned out to be quite profitable; I had no real overhead costs and a captured hungry market.

The enterprise was short-lived because I was asked to stop selling food on or around the school grounds, but by then it had sparked a real interest in business and the simplicity of selling. It was simple: just giving people what they wanted. That early experience wasn't really selling; it was just matching something to someone that wanted it. I just put the sandwich in easy reach of the hungry school kid. That idea is the foundation of all good sales: sell something to people that want or need it. It was to be the first of several home enterprises that I got involved with, always with the simple idea of selling what people actually wanted. I wasn't a salesperson to the people that bought from me. I was the kid that sold huge sandwiches, or the kid that sold video and computer games. I never saw it as selling or as being a salesperson; it was just something I was doing and actually had fun doing, and this is the distinction: I was having fun. I did it because I could, because I wanted to and not with the idea that it was just the money I was after.

I had always been interested in science and medicine, and for a short while at school I had the idea of a career in pathology but with less than a natural aptitude for chemistry and disappointing school grades, I settled for two weeks' work experience in the microbiology department of the local hospital. As much as I enjoyed it, I never saw myself as a lab technician and so the idea of a future in medicine quickly dissolved and I went off to college. I took a course in business and economics but I wasn't a particularly academic student. I left college three years later with ok grades and little idea as to what I was going to do next. I was like most others of my age, enthusiastic and excited to see what the world might have in store for me. It wasn't long after leaving college that a friend offered me a few days' work helping out with a stocktake at a nearby scuba diving store. I had been a keen scuba diver since the age of 15 and whilst counting wetsuits and masks wasn't the most varied work one might imagine for a recent college leaver, it was only a few days and I was pretty interested in the different types of equipment they sold so, with nothing else to do that week, I jumped at the chance.

As it happened those three days' work ended up being over three years. I sort of became a sales assistant at the Diving Locker, West London, and I loved it. For an 18-year-old at the time, it never really felt like work to me because I simply loved diving. I loved talking about diving, learning more about the industry, equipment and the environment. I was always eager to learn about new equipment, how it worked, and to share the benefit of that knowledge with customers when they visited the store. The selling part just seemed to happen. I was never really attached to the outcome; I just assumed they wanted to buy something and quite often they did. I just talked with the customers about diving and dive trips, simply asking them about their diving experiences, what their level was, where they were going, together with what they needed from the kit they sought to buy. I was able to match those needs to the right equipment discovered from the fun conversations I had with the customers, but to me it was just talking about diving.

The store carried a wide array of brands and I loved learning about all of them. How things like demand valves and buoyancy jackets worked. The more I learnt about it the more I was able to help customers choose the best equipment for their specific needs. A year after I joined the Diving Locker the business was bought by Ocean Leisure, a bigger store based in central London. My enthusiasm and performance were noticed and I suddenly found myself working at the flagship store in London Embankment and I soon became responsible for the diving and watersports department.

By then I was 20 and in charge of training new sales assistants on the equipment we sold, but that also included how to engage with customers, getting them to open up about what they wanted so that we could ensure we offered them exactly what they needed. I had no formal sales training but I knew that connecting with the customer, asking the right questions and listening to their answers was the key to being successful, which is why in those early days I was really successful in what I did. My approach to selling, knowing my products, connecting with customers and asking the right questions together with paying careful attention to their responses was, and has remained, the foundation of my sales career and the success I have experienced.

Over the next 20 years the environments I sold into changed considerably. I refined my understanding of the sales process and I learnt new approaches to sales engagement but fundamentally the foundation has never changed. Match the product with a person that needs or wants it, listen to what they say and always try to give them want they want. Beyond that I have also come to realise that enthusiasm for what I did contributed significantly to the successes throughout my career.

The importance of enthusiasm or energetic state and its role in being successful is abundantly clear to me, something to be covered in Part 2. During those early years in the diving industry my energy – or, as I now see it, my energetic state – played such an important role in how events unfolded. My love of diving and engaging with people in the shop environment allowed me to flow with what we look upon as high energy in my work. That enthusiasm becomes evident to those you come into contact with too, because it is a magnetic attractive quality, drawing people to you.

One particular summer's day at Ocean Leisure I served a gentleman in his late fifties. I probably spent a couple of hours in the store with him in total. As I recall he was buying a lot of equipment for himself and his family; the sale was to run into the thousands of pounds. I don't really remember the interaction, only the outcome. When all was done I finally rang up the total and he paid the bill. With all the bags he had filled, he asked me to help him on the street so he could hail a taxi. Whilst waiting for a cab he turned to me and rather bluntly asked me what I made as a salary working at Ocean Leisure. I was a little surprised but answered him nonetheless. I still remember his response very clearly: "We pay our secretaries more than that", with an air of surprise and pomp. He proceeded to explain that he was the managing director of a family owned private medical healthcare company and to my surprise he offered me a job. I wasn't prepared for that, nor did I really understand what he was offering, but I agreed to spend a day at his Baker Street offices visiting the different departments and meeting the staff.

Looking back, visiting the offices was pretty overwhelming. Compared to the dive store this was big business, a far departure from the retail diving environment I came from. At the end of the day there I sat down with Ernie Brett, the MD, in his office and we discussed my role. He wanted me to be what he described as his right hand, to learn all about the business and, if it were to work out, to take a managerial role within the firm. It is clear now he was offering me mentorship and what we might look upon today as a management fast track position. He joked that I could do very well there but I would never be a company director as my name wasn't Brett. I was being offered a huge opportunity, with double the salary I was currently making, a real opportunity to learn about business, about the medical insurance business, which is where it started to unravel for me. You see, I just could not get excited about the business, and maybe naively I didn't appreciate the role for what I could make it but as a 20-year-old I just felt it was too dull compared to the way that the dive industry made me feel. I thanked him for his offer and said I would think about it over the weekend. I never went back.

I do believe, and I have said this before, that every situation, every moment is imbued with a kind of *super potentiality*, an idea that there exists the possibility of many other outcomes being possible beyond the one which is immediately obvious in any given moment. The day that E.B. Brett visited our store I had no idea what was to come from the interaction with this quirky old man buying dive equipment for his family. I just approached him like any other customer, with genuine enthusiasm and a desire to serve, to make sure he got what he needed. I didn't contain it; I was just enthusiastically being me.

That behaviour, of being in service to your client, speaks loud and clear, which perhaps is why this successful businessman looked beyond the outward appearance of a 20-year-old with a ponytail working in a dive store and saw something more, maybe sensing the potentiality that at the time I had not considered. Until the time of writing this I had hardly thought of that story; it happened such a long time ago but I doubt I will forget it. It made me see that the most unlikely things are possible from the most everyday situations. If the experience and others like it have taught me anything, it is not to reduce the present moment to the mundane by looking at it as undesirable or less important than some other imagined future moment. Not to see the future as better, or more opportunistic than this moment, because it is only this moment that things happen. You simply never know whom you might encounter or what your true impact is upon the world around you.

Not taking the job was the right decision for the 20-year-old me. As it happened, a few months later I was to leave my job at Ocean Leisure and go out to the United States, broadening my horizons and enjoying some diving in the warm waters of the Florida Keys that many of the customers I served had spoken about during my time at the dive shop.

We are where we are in our life situation, in this very moment, thanks to every step we have taken in the past – or in this instance I didn't take. On a few occasions I have wondered where I might have ended up if I had taken that job, but never from a sense of missing out, simply curiosity of where it might have taken me. I never consciously chose a sales career; it just happened that each of the experiences and jobs and environments I found myself in, in some way equipped me with skills and experience that aligned me with a successful career in sales. The routine and yet varied world of retail served me hugely as it was from within that environment that I got a sense of people and how to read them, encountering all manner of personalities and situations, not all of them fun, but all adding to the wealth of data we subconsciously draw upon to frame our perspective of the world as we see it.

After my time in the US, I returned to the UK, finding some work for a short while with a direct to consumer cell phone provider within the logistics team before returning to the diving industry. I joined a professional diving company that worked with film production companies. It was amazing fun and something that I enjoyed immensely, with varied and exciting projects. However, not long after starting this role and being on location in Ireland for a few months, I returned home and suddenly felt that I wanted to do something different. As much as I enjoyed what I had been doing I wanted to make more permanent roots so decided to make a change. With the last contract finished I started to look for a new job. I was 25 and I didn't have much in the way of academic qualifications but that never really bothered me. I always felt my strengths came through when I was face to face and felt if I could get an interview I would somehow be fine.

Back then it was still very normal to search for jobs in newspapers and I found myself circling a number of jobs including some sales roles that sounded quite interesting. Eventually after many applications and few responses I got an interview with a company that manufactured medical equipment. They were growing and looking for an on-the-road territory sales rep. The medical company job was my first real sales role, defined as having a territory, monthly sales targets and the opportunity to earn more than just a base salary. I stayed there two years. I did ok, made most of my targets and some good commissions but I didn't excel, and perhaps that in part was the environment and not fully appreciating the way sales got made in the UK NHS.

Technically I was quite proficient, and understood a lot about the micro video camera systems we sold, but at 25 I wasn't as comfortable in the environment as I had been within the diving industry. I never really felt I was able to connect with the buyers, who were almost always surgeons, in the way that I had within the diving environment, or as well as other more successful reps did, and because of that I never saw it as a long-term role. It was clear that those connections, those relationships, were a huge aspect of success and without them it was a lot more challenging to be successful, not just with targets but my own personal sense of success.

We measure the quality of the relationships we build; it might be a reflection of how easy or difficult getting access to our client is. When they take the call it reflects the idea that there is a perceived benefit from doing so, that there exists to some degree an appreciation for the value that you and your services or products deliver. These details contribute to the way we evaluate the challenge and our progress with completing it. So after two years of never really feeling like I fitted in, not being particularly comfortable with my clients, I decided to look for another job.

I secured an appointment with a recruitment consultant who specialised in the medical sales and technology environments, thinking maybe different products to a different type of end client would allow me to build more of that feeling of connection that I so effortlessly had within the diving world. I hadn't considered changing industry, only the company, but within a few minutes of arriving for the consult I was being told I was "all wrong" for medical sales, and that I should consider the world of ISP sales, selling Internet services to businesses. If I am honest about it I was a little relieved to hear that maybe the medical equipment environment was not a match for me, but I guess that's the ego not wanting to be wrong about what we can and can't be successful at.

Nonetheless I was intrigued to hear more about a role within the world of Internet sales. At that time the Internet was still a relatively new thing. It was the year 2000; home access to the web was through modem dial-up at the blistering speed of 56k. Google had only launched in 1998, and Facebook wasn't to appear for another four years; yes it was early on in this new and exciting industry and I sensed the opportunity. I interviewed successfully for a small regional ISP. I was to be selling fixed lease line Internet access with speeds that seem comical today, ranging from 64kbps to 2mbps. By comparison, today my 4G mobile phone service is around 100mbps.

This was indeed the early days of a brave new world and the geeky part of me that loved diving and the equipment instantly recognised the pull of the technology we were to be offering and what it could enable. Here was an environment I could feel excited about again. I made sure that I knew as much as I could about the services we offered, the environment in which we worked and how it solved problems for clients. That enthusiasm for what we were doing, the solving of customer problems, connecting them to this paradigm-changing web of information and having fun with it at the same time, is probably a large part of why I was very successful.

A decade later, still within the telecommunications industry, I unexpectedly found myself being asked to manage a team of young salespeople for a company that built, owned and operated fibre optics data networks across the US and London. The management of other salespeople was not something I had given any thought to. In fact at first I was quite resistant to the idea, but presented with a very persuasive offer and more than a little curiosity as to where it might lead, I agreed. It was there that I started to notice the elements of behaviour consistently observed in successful performance. Not that I was immediately aware of it in those terms, nor was it just the presence of commercial acumen exhibited, but it was also evident in mindset traits present amongst those within my team and in the wider company who, like members of the team, excelled in what they did, contributing greatly to the success of the company in the space we played.

But before we go further into those traits, let us revisit the original question of why you became a sales professional. Were you like me: simply stumbling your way into it, thinking it was something that you could do for a while until you had a clearer idea about what you really wanted to do?

For those that hold a clear account of their why, does that why still underpin the *how* you serve your customers and clients each day? Is there still an underlying enthusiasm for why you spend a large portion of your waking day as you do, getting up each morning ready to solve problems and deliver solutions? Or has that enthusiasm given way to the practical demands of daily life and the need to earn sufficiently in order to enjoy the lifestyle you have created? If so, how did this happen; did you wake up one day with a different outlook?

I dare say for many much time has passed since the enthusiastic beginnings of their sales career. As time passes we tend to seek out ways to simplify the things done frequently. We naturally form routines to manage many repetitive aspects of our life. Who goes into the bathroom first in the morning, who does the shopping and when, or when we choose to go to the gym each week. It's habitual and it makes meeting those tasks, responsibilities and actions all the more manageable, as it all fits into the organised world we create for ourselves. And so as days pass into months and years within our careers those same routines take shape.

In the sales environment the routine is structural to the working week, with certain functions that must be met like the administrative aspects of the job, the prospecting, the sales funnel update and the data entry of new opportunities. Then there is the weekly or monthly sales meeting, reviewing live opportunities, calling the ones which will drop, slip or have gone away. These activities form the structure to the working week. This is normal: it's efficiency of action and energy intended to move you from where you are to the next step in the sales process, but it is also the way in which we can fall into a rut.

Of course in amongst the daily and weekly workflow there does exist variation. Client-centric activities like meetings and telephone calls are varied by their very nature: interactions with differing people, companies and opportunities. Those activities point to the opportunity for variation but that variety may only exist on the client side if the salesperson meets those situations with the same approach and thought patterns towards the possible outcomes each time.

New engagements with prospective clients can quite easily cover the same ground each time, with the delivery of a perfectly crafted story or following a series of steps in the meeting to arrive at where you need to be in order to progress to the next stage. How often do you examine and change your value proposition when meeting with clients? If you do find yourself repeating the same engagement pattern every time, you are likely to elicit the same outcomes with clients and prospects.

I am not saying there is complacency in this behaviour, more that with the proficiency of doing these tasks every day the practicality of aspects of the work can become automatic. I am simply inviting you to bring awareness to the area of client engagement: look at what you communicate and how it is delivered. Do you ever adjust, vary or modify those core messages? There is confidence in familiarity; we can comfortably deliver a well-rehearsed value proposition to anyone. Owning the words can make it all the more impactful but it can also create a situation where it stops being a dialogue intended to open discussion and simply a means of telling your story. Seasoned salespeople can develop a strong sense of the opportunity potential very quickly, making judgements on the situation based on the experienced gained over the years.

I have always held great value in strong qualification but how quickly does qualification give way to opinion, a judgement that draws on experiences of other meetings, companies or potential opportunities encountered in the past? How many of those experiences colour the way the moment is perceived? Is that at all possible for you? If you examine your own experiences, have you ever had the feeling in those very early moments of a meeting or call where you felt you knew where things were heading, without necessarily having any tangible reason to believe the judgement to be true, just that your gut feeling or past experiences lit up a few warning lights about what was unfolding? If that is at all possible then is it also possible that you stopped qualifying the opportunity and started unconsciously validating those feelings, whatever they might be, looking for further evidence in the responses given? The moment we start thinking about the opportunity whilst with the client, even if the thoughts are vaguely forming in the back of the mind, we are drawing from the subconsciously held bank of experiences. When that happens we have left the present moment and the client connection to draw upon thoughts and ideas from the past.

Does such proficiency and experience put us in danger of losing some of our objectivity? Occasionally expecting certain outcomes from situations simply because they have the look and feel of familiarity? We start to size up companies, people and potential opportunities very quickly, commonly because time is a precious resource so there is an underlying desire to limit wasting valuable time in situations that will not profit us or further the meeting of our sales targets. If we allow the first impression of the opportunity or situation to influence the way we evaluate opportunity, we run the risk of looking for evidence to validate and reinforce the judgement we make at the expense of opening up the dialogue sufficiently to deliver a solution, solve a problem and build a relationship with the client.

In those meetings, where we have maybe quickly decided there is no immediate value, are we just looking to finish the meeting and get back to the office? I know I have been in that situation throughout my career. It's a tough one; at times if I didn't feel there was sufficient alignment between my wants and the needs or client's current situation then suddenly I would become aware of other more pressing matters that my time could be directed towards, drawing me further away from the present moment with the client and the opportunity for connection. It may well be that there is little or no opportunity immediately present or in the near future, but how the meeting unfolds and the attention you direct to it will have an impact on how you are received and perceived.

As much as we like to think of ourselves as being able to maintain a poker face, masking what we really think, I wonder how many of our ideas and thoughts about the meeting and potential opportunity spill out to be picked up on by the other party at some subconscious level? In more recent times, scientists have realised that the electrical currents occurring naturally in the brain can be read in the magnetic "field" outside of our body. This might sound strange but the work of molecular biologist Bruce Lipton seems to point to the reality that, as individuals, our thoughts are constantly creating this electromagnetic field which stretches well beyond the borders of our body in the form of electromagnetic radiation, which can be measured with a medical device called an MEG or magnetoencephalogram. Now there might not currently be evidence to prove that those waves are interpretable at a conscious level by those around us, but subconsciously perhaps. After all, what is it that creates our feelings about first impressions?

In a broader sense, the possibility of losing our creativity found in the variety of experiences in favour of a more automatic reaction puts us at risk of losing touch with a clear sense of the underlying WHY that started us on this path all those years ago. Just for clarity, I mean the WHY beyond the obvious need to earn money in order to function in society. It may well surprise you to learn that around 95% of our mental activity, of our cognitive function, is under the veil of our conscious awareness, including our deepest drivers, motivations and beliefs. Our subconscious continues to shape our lives and the version of ourselves we show the world. When we practise activities frequently eventually they move from our conscious mind into the subconscious, and we no longer need to give the same conscious awareness to the execution and thus the activity becomes automatic.

If you learnt to ride a bike or drive a car, in the beginning learning the mechanics of the activity required your full conscious focus of what you were doing to learn the new skills. Then as proficiency was gained and the new skills integrated, the activity was carried out automatically. You suddenly stop paying conscious attention to the *how* you are doing it and redirect your conscious attention to a different horizon, such as navigating the terrain rather than balancing the bike. So why should the way we work be any different?

Once we have acquired the practical skills we pay less attention to the *what* we are doing in order to focus on the landscape we are working within and we become goal orientated, so as to focus on where we want to get to rather than where we are.

The success to be found within each and every moment lies within the awareness of that moment: paying attention to the person, situation and environment without presuming to know the full potential of the moment. Listening to what is being said, responding to what is needed, rather than allowing a limited idea to form because there may be aspects of the situation that are similar to previous meetings, people and opportunities that turned out to have little or no value. I am not saying ignore what your experience has brought you but don't colour the present moment with the judgements of a previous meeting. Ask questions, listen to the answers given and proceed according to what is best for the expansion of the conversation. If after the discussion there remain gaps in the criteria from which you evaluate the opportunity then proceed on that basis, but the challenge here is to be aware of where your ideas come from, to allow the conversation to unfold without making punctuated judgements as the conversation progresses such that you run the risk of looking for validations for your judgement rather than a deeper understanding of the potential fit for a working solution to be successfully presented and received.

In the purest sense of the sales role, the salesperson is there balancing the interests of the client, by finding solutions to the obstacles to their business's growth and success, with the opposing side of the scale, meeting their employer's sales targets, growing market share and promoting their products or services. After all, isn't that what we were taught in our early sales career? Discover our customer's biggest problem, match it with the best solution, and then negotiate the winning price to close the sale. It's the win–win outcome we all seek; after all, you want the customer to be happy with the decision, right? Right? I mean that is what you consciously believe and pursue.

What you ultimately want is for your client to be happy with the decision to buy from you, or is your why about you selling to them, so you can make money? Maybe you see it as the same thing, but is it the same? Maybe it's closer to reality that when you stop seeing your clients as a means to make money, they will stop seeing you as someone trying to take it from them. That change requires an attitudinal shift, a getting back to basics as to what you are about as a salesperson.

I remember as a young salesman undertaking sales training courses, and listening to my manager I was told, "Ask questions about what keeps the customer awake at night about their business". We needed to find out what was stopping them from achieving their objectives, as a company and as an individual, and we were told to understand the personal wins of our contact and help them achieve them. In other words, make our client look good by providing them with the solution which would make them look good.

In the prevailing reality we are employed to sell our services and products to clients likely to want and need them, so in a sense this engagement translates to being in service to our customers, solving their problems, adding value to their business, and along the way if successful in helping our clients we will receive a reward for the performance of that service, which we receive as a salary and a commission together with the non-tangible aspects of the reward such as recognition and praise.

It also stands true that if we flip the coin, the reverse of being in service to our clients is to be in service to our employer too. We represent the company and its interests through our continued engagement with the marketplace, and yes the exchange of our energy and time is for a salary and commission, but it is still a service we perform, promoting our company and its services. Or do we? I mean that's what is supposed to drive each of us in our profession, right? However the answer is likely to be a more personal reason, dare it even be said that what drives us, our "why", is selfish motivations, such as money, recognition and status. Of the salespeople going to work every day, how many are thinking about how they can better serve their customers and employers?

Maybe the "why" in what we do has a major impact on how we do what we do, and if there is a how there must be a what. Does the how and what change when we lose sight of the why? Could it be that the more lofty the cause, the more the WHY and then the WHAT and HOW are somehow altered? Do we take more care, showing greater attention to the detail, when the why is important to us, when we have a personal resonance with the cause?

How much time is put into the creation of a resume or CV for a job application? The fact that an industry exists to provide this professional service is a reflection of the value we place on securing the right jobs, so we invest more of our resources into the creation of something (our resume or CV) in order to help us secure an interview. We invest in an aspect of the process, which can be translated to the what and how – through the use of a professional resume service, or by spending our own time crafting the right content which is driven by the underlying why.

Looking back over the interviews in the early days of my career, I was asked why I wanted to work at that company. I cannot honestly say I remember exactly, but likely I would have given polished rehearsed responses. Ones about working for a progressive company, that the industry really engaged me, and that I really thrived working in challenging competitive environments such as corporate sales. Those were all sincere replies but I can't actually recall, which is not to say it never came up, but I can't actually recall ever saying I wanted to be in service to the clients they served. It now becomes clearer to me that I see the difference between being of service and serving myself. Maybe it takes the perspective of time to arrive at that awareness or it's simply a matter of exploring the underlying motivations. Either way now it is clear that a lot of what I did in my career was undertaken with a sense of what it would give me. There is nothing wrong with that; I do not judge myself harshly, nor anyone else for that matter. Neither does that mean that the work that I did was of a poor quality; it just means that on reflection it was not about being in service to my clients or even my employer. It was serving myself and with that stance seeing the world in adversarial terms, where I am either winning or losing, was a natural modality to operate with.

Many years ago I was working for a growing European Internet services provider. We worked in East London in a large data centre where a few floors were office space but the majority of the building floors were dedicated to securely housing the IT infrastructure of our customers. In the second year I uncovered an opportunity for a large company that provided pre-paid calling cards, the sort that let you call the other side of the world at a fraction of the normal cost. They were interested in some space within the data centre. The initial deal itself wasn't huge but a presales colleague uncovered a greater technical need within the company and from there I went on to develop an opportunity that became huge.

At that time it was the biggest co-location and interconnect deal the company had seen and I was driving it. In truth it was very much a team effort and I was as clear about that at the time as I am today. The difference was, back then, I was focused entirely on what the deal meant to me financially. I was 28 years old and the deal represented something like £50,000 in commission. I was looking at how I might buy a sky blue convertible Lamborghini, or a property of my own. The thoughts of what closing the piece of business meant were intoxicating and motivating all of my actions. It was the thought that got me to work early each morning, and had me working late at night. I was driven and hungry.

Of course I wanted the customer to be happy because I saw that as a requisite component in obtaining my desired outcome. Again many may read this and not see any problem in this modality, and there is nothing wrong per se. However, for me client satisfaction with the solution just represented something that needed to be in place in order for our proposal to be selected which would provide me with what I wanted, namely the commission and kudos, rather than wanting to do the best for the client and my employer because that was why I was employed. In truth I am not convinced my employer saw it any differently; I was employed to win contracts and help the company grow.

However we are more likely to gain respect, loyalty and more trust from our customers if they truly believe we are out to help them achieve their goals rather than just trying to sell them a solution. If you are sincere with that intention then your authenticity will shine more clearly and that authenticity is important, as coming from authenticity will engender trust, and from trust you can build loyalty, and why is loyalty important? Because loyalty is the difference between choosing to work with a salesperson to find the solution together even if they end up being more expensive than another similar solution offered more cheaply by a competitor.

If we perceive a greater value in the cause of what we do, are we not inspired to go to greater lengths to make good the outcome, to invest greater care and attention to the ingredients of whatever we cook up?

There are several fundamental points which will come as little surprise to anyone reading this. I have said before that an essential part of us achieving our objectives is around the efficacy of our communication and for communication to happen there must be one who speaks and another who listens. I am fairly certain for most salespeople that the speaking part is not the problem. From the time we join our employer we are educated and trained to speak, giving out the value proposition, which has been carefully crafted to increase the likelihood of the client identifying with the company and solution in front of them.

The roles we play

All too often and in the wider sense of society, people adopt roles and nearly always unconsciously. In fact it is inevitable. We are assigned our most basic roles at birth, such as the role of son or daughter, our nationality and in many cases our religion. If you were born in France you cannot without considerable change to your situation and circumstances say that you are German, or if you were born a Christian it is not very likely you will ever see yourself as being Muslim. As for gender, you are born a male or female and from there, for each of those labels, those designations, you adopt a prescribed and well defined sense of what that means. Our gender to a major extent defines the type of clothing that we wear, the sports we play and the way we express ourselves. Then as we develop and grow we start to adopt other roles, some as a matter of social engineering, such as the popular culture prevalent at the time, the music we follow or any other external identity which can be overlaid on the self and from which a sense of identify can be derived.

Why are these roles? Well, they are roles because they are the results of ideas we hold about ourselves when we start to associate the idea with who we are. There are countless roles we play every day: we play the parent, the commuter, the customer in the coffee shop, we play the employee, the account manager. We play many roles, and before you decide if that is you or not, ask yourself one simple question: is the person you are turning up as in every one of these situations the same? Are you authentically you; do you treat every situation and interaction the same? Do you engage with your client the way you engage with the waiter in a restaurant? If you don't then in what way are you being different in each and every situation? Are you adopting a different tone, attitude or demeanour with each? If you do change yourself with your audience then which one is the real you, and if the other person is not getting the real you, is it conceivable that you are not getting the real them, the authentic them?

So it's the adoption of roles in the corporate environment that can be a major barrier to communication and the building of relationships: you are being the account manager and they are being the customer rather than simply two people engaging. Think about it for a moment before reading on.

Do you have a sense of what you SHOULD be like in the execution of your duties as a salesperson?

Moving away from labels

There is a benefit for all of us in moving away from attachment and identification with the labels commonplace in business and in society as a whole. Labelling stuff just covers over the truth of the matter, and that truth, in the context of being in service to your clients, is that your opportunity to serve is far greater when things are going wrong. The trouble is when "things" go wrong in a business environment there are numerous elements influencing the way in which the situation is addressed. This is totally opposite to what the majority of people feel energetically in the moment.

What is far more common an interpretation is that the issue creates a sense of risk, a fear of loss, which often lurks beneath the surface because regardless of actual cause it is quite normal to fear judgement from a multitude of angles, judgement from the client, from your own organisation and of course judgement of yourself and your ability to deal with what has arisen. So often it is the case that these feelings/emotions are subliminally experienced, or not; it can be quite evident that the judgements are being made. Irrespective of this the net effect is there is a lessening of your energy and a possible lowering of your state. The bigger the client and their respective problem the greater the energetic consequence. It's because we perceive them as big clients or see the issue as looming large on the horizon that it registers as it does. It's because we have invested some degree of our sense of self with the clients we have. We hold the idea of our success as salespeople in the acquisition of more contracts and more clients. This is why we are so easily affected because the challenge to our client in the issue that has manifested at some level challenges our sense of self; it challenges our idea that we are being successful salespeople.

If you pitched and subsequently won five really prestigious large ticket clients you would be hard pushed not to experience a sense of achievement and in all likelihood enjoy the feeling of that success being reflected to you by your peers and leaders, so if your sense of achievement is so enhanced by the acquisition of said clients, does it not follow that the inverse would also be true? Would you not feel smaller if you were to lose those clients for whatever reason? And it's this reductionism of our self that I want to get to the heart of in this section. You and I are both already completely successful in so many ways, but because of societal and commercial conditioning we have a very narrow framework to reference and measure our "success". The entire content of this book has been placed before you to encourage you to think and perceive differently such that you can experience greater success in your career. It's not what is outside of you that influences success.

So going back to the big issue and the important client, rather obviously the most pressing thing is to solve the problem, remove the issue and return things to a normal operating service. And for the salesperson that can remain dispassionate in their interpretation and interaction with the variables in play, it becomes an activity like any other. There will be things that need to be done and challenges to the achievement of those activities.

Chapter Summary

How to be in Service to Your Clients

- Engage totally and fully with the action in the moment, not as a step to where you want to be, such as a next meeting, presentation or the signing of a contract. Be engaged with what is happening now.
- Sales opportunities are a journey, so make your client's destination that of your own.
- Be clear about your why. Align your what and how with your why to be congruent in what you do.
- Let go of any ideas about yourself, and whatever is left is the authentic you.

Chapter 4 – Consistency

This book is concerned with fostering greater success in your sales experiences. If there is one thing I am sure of, which has been repeated to me by my mentor, it is that success leaves clues. So as a foundation to building understanding and making accessible the benefit within the Points of Conscious Performance, I want to share a few insights with you about successful people.

We never really have far to look in order to recognise them. Simply put, consistency is a fundamental attribute shown in their behaviour, and it can be found everywhere we see exceptional performance. It's like the former manager of Arsenal football club Arsene Wenger said: "When you look at people who are successful, you will find that they aren't the people who are motivated, but have consistency in their motivation."

It is not just within the sporting world that this view is held. It can be observed in the corporate arenas just as clearly. "Success is neither magical nor mysterious. Success is the natural consequence of consistently applying basic fundamentals," says Jim Rohn (rags to riches American entrepreneur). In fact, according to Google, when hiring for leaders, the most important quality looked for in a candidate is consistency. So consistency is of key importance, but how does this get noticed? What are the positive consequences of consistency to those around you? To answer this we can look to our colleagues as well as our clients but maybe, before we can answer that question adequately, we need to ask what we mean by consistency.

Consistency of what exactly? As a starting point let's look at the most frequently occurring variable in the equation, which is you! It is really a case of consistency in being you. As we touched upon in the last section, the way you show up at your workplace, the way your clients see you in meetings or the way you greet the person in the coffee shop each morning, if they don't all see the same person, are you really being authentically you? Do you ever notice your language change or perhaps your attitude changes occasionally or frequently for that matter, depending on your audience? Perhaps other external factors play a role.

From time to time many people are affected to varying degrees by a multitude of external things. These little bumps are quite often beyond our control and they seem to spring up at the most inopportune times. Things like the changeable British weather having the power to affect some people's outlook simply because they have to walk in the rain to the metro. Perhaps the parking ticket when they were only a few minutes over time. For many people the daily commute dampens the spirit, especially when it involves using overcrowded public transport.

If we allow external factors to change our outlook, in that moment it means we are operating with an affected state, a lowered inner energy. We are not seeing the world with our normal outlook. This change in attitude towards what is perceived can also subtly change the way we interact with the people we encounter, that's to say it impacts the version of you they and the world see. If how you are perceived can be affected by the way you feel in any given moment, a change in your state potentially brought about by external events happening around you, then have you considered how consistent you are? What might that be influencing in the mind of the other person in any situation, from the ticket inspector at the train station to the client at your first meeting of the day?

Over the years in each company I found myself working with people who showed up day in and day out with an almost constant "get on with it" attitude. They were always helpful and would approach their work and whatever challenges came up with this "get on with it" engaging attitude. They were what we might commonly describe as "professional" in the execution of their work, but it appeared to be deeper than that. Yes, they were indeed professional in the way in which they went about their work, but there seemed to exist within them an engaging, positive outlook to whatever came up.

For example, as a salesman, once a deal had been signed it was necessary to work with a project manager and the client to ensure the services were delivered according to what had been agreed. It's fair to say that in one particular company there was strong competition to work with certain PMs simply because it was apparent that projects got delivered to a higher satisfaction for our clients with those PMs. In the world of telecoms, when delivering Wide Area Voice and Data Networks there were frequently unforeseen or unavoidable occurrences arising which created delays and challenges, and it was in those situations that the difference between project managers became evident. It is when things go wrong that we have the greatest opportunity to serve clients and I observed a consistency in the engagement and state of these particular project managers. The same positive enthusiasm that was present at the first post-signature meeting between the clients and the PM remained even when things went wrong. What was noticeable was the trust that was quickly established between the client and the PM because there was a consistency of performance and state demonstrated by the PM.

That consistency of performance, as simple as always calling with updates as promised even if it was with less than great news, is still a constant that can be relied upon. When people do what they say they will consistently, trust is more easily established. They are perceived as reliable, because they show themselves to be someone less likely to be affected by bumps in the road. Things happen and they adjust what they do and continue with the same focus directed to the desired outcome. There were many instances where clients commented on the difference in their experiences with project managers from different organisations. Generally people with a consistent demeanour and outlook are far more memorable and stand out, so are more likely to build deeper business relationships with the trust of their peers and colleagues compared to someone whose response to adversity is to complain, point a finger or become hard to reach.

The same could be applied to you and your clients. Is it reasonable to conclude that the account manager showing up every time possessing that same "can-do" client-centric competence, one who is consistent in everything they do for the client, would be most likely to engender trust, a sense of reliability and confidence? Yes, this is professionalism but the energy from which that professionalism emanates – their energetic state – plays a significant role in how that person performs and how they are perceived. A positive trait like consistency of energetic state present in a person's demeanour, in the way they are being with what they are doing, is more likely to have a positive lasting impact in terms of the way they are seen and engaged with by colleagues and clients.

Chapter Summary

Consistency

- Be consistent in who you show up as each day.
- Deliver on your promises every day.
- Turn up each day with the same "can-do" client-centric desire to serve.
- If you notice things in another person, could it be a reflection of you? Pay attention to what is around you.

Chapter 5 – Introducing the Points of Conscious Performance

These following chapters are intended to promote and encourage you to approach your sales activities, your client relationship development, in fact every aspect of what you do in your working lives with a deeper *conscious awareness*. In doing so you will be bringing in another dimension to the developed art of your sales engagement. So what is conscious awareness when applied to the sales environment? It is actually rather simple; to be consciously aware in the sale is to be completely focused on the activity you are engaged in at any given moment. It is when your attention is fully given over to whatever it is you are working on or whoever you are working with. When your focus is centred upon where you are in the very moment, in what you are engaged in, you are in the present moment with what you are doing. That state is reflective of a mind fully employed for the specific task.

An example, albeit an obvious one, might be when you're making a call to a client, meaning the call is the sole focus of your mental activity. In that moment you are actively listening to the voice of your client, taking in what is being said, not just waiting for a pause in their flow in order to speak. Being consciously aware on a call means that your mind is free from thoughts of what to have for lunch, thinking about the game last night or any other related or unrelated thoughts that may be floating around in the back of your mind at any given time. Sounds obvious? Ok, what about when you're entering data into your Customer Relationship Management tool (CRM) or any other routine activity; can you say you are always focused on correctly entering the information? You could be engaged in any activity when your attention might flit between different points of focus. Maybe whilst entering information you're having a conversation with someone sitting across the desk from you which from moment to moment takes some or all of your attention away from the task at hand.

There are countless opportunities within the office and beyond to be distracted from the task at hand in our daily working lives. How much mental activity is expended on non-productive pursuits or distracting you from the task at hand? Take driving to and from the sales appointment: when you are driving, how much of the driving is automatic and how much of your mind's attention is elsewhere? Are you thinking about the meeting you are going to have rather than paying attention to the road?

How much more productive could we be if we could focus entirely on what we are supposed to be doing at any given time? This isn't about being a robot; it's about making the most of, and engaging thoroughly with, the task. It's about being productive and focused on work when you are working such that you lose yourself in what you are doing. There are plenty of opportunities for your mind to indulge ideas about lunch, discuss the game with your colleagues or shoot the breeze on your breaks.

Now, taking consistency as a basic underlying principle, before we dive in any deeper it may be helpful to offer an introduction to each of the three Points of Conscious Performance, or to put it differently, the forces at work which have the potential to alter the outcome of the situations and events beyond our immediate perception. State, intention and belief are first and foremost aspects of the self that with awareness make it possible for each and every one of us to realise more success in the things we choose to undertake. This is made possible through changes to the way we perceive and interact with the world around us. Although they each interact and interlace with each other we can look upon state as the starting point and foundation to our further understanding.

State

In simple terms state is a description of something quite intangible and yet we are able to feel it in others as moods or energies, and when we become aware we can notice it in ourselves. It's the energy of our animated being, the life force that pervades the entire body. It is how one feels in any given moment. Your state affects how you see the world around you, playing a role in determining what is perceived as possible and which successes are achievable in your own mind. Upon realising those higher states can positively influence the way we see things, the importance of state maintenance becomes quickly recognisable because our life experiences are a series of decisions made based on our own interpretation of events unfolding around us. A low state can render someone drained of vitality and unable to realise his or her desired goals and targets and therefore slowed by every obstacle encountered. Conversely high energy, high state individuals find a path through whatever it is that is unfolding , responding consciously to whatever is needed from them in that moment to bring about a fix to the situation or to move quickly beyond whatever event is encountered, however unexpected that might be.

Intention

What we sense as being possible for us to accomplish in life and indeed our careers is heavily influenced by our state but that sense of what is possible needs to be acted upon; there must be action. Action takes you from your current situation to a desired outcome, but that desired outcome must be clearly stated. It must be recognisable as a destination arrived at through the direction of your actions, because without direction, driven by set intentions, the prevailing patterns of your subconscious past experiences will run as a default deciding for you a destination, and not necessarily the destination you want.

Without set intentions the mind will draw from past experiences in order to frame present moment interpretation. Without intentions activity is driven by the programming of subconscious, mostly invisible ideas and beliefs about yourself and whatever you are engaged in.

We will go on to explore how setting strong enabling intentions can start to change some of the unconscious patterns of behaviour you may come to observe in yourself, together with how those patterns of behaviour influence the results you encounter, discovering what happens when you leave it to chance and the benefits of incorporating intention setting into your daily practices.

Belief

The final part of the trinity is the means by which we pay for our desired success with our belief acting as currency, meeting the price of our endeavours, especially in the face of adversity. This enables us to overcome those moments when we consider giving up but find the strength to continue. Belief catalyses the power of state and intention to bring about the energy we draw down on and the drive needed to accomplish the things we set our sights on. The greater the challenge the greater the correspondent belief in the outcome must be present to overcome the inertia encountered by some when things get difficult or at first seem impossible. We will examine the components of our creativity, understanding how to access the power available to us through congruency of our thoughts, words and actions, anchoring within us the belief that what we seek to accomplish is achievable and within reach.

Part 2 – State

State forms the underlying foundation of all your experiences as it can influence the filter through which you perceive your life events happening, and it is the essence of what this book is about. It's the basis for the experience of success in your working life, determining what you see and how you respond, and to a large extent is the energetic force determining the way you interact with whatever you are doing in the present moment. So what is it? How is it reflected in each of us? State is really our inner condition, how we are feeling inside, often apparent to others but not limited to outward appearance. It is the feeling of how we are doing inside, ranging from a sense of what is possible to what frame of mind we or another might be experiencing, and is a true reflection of our wellbeing. It shapes how we engage with activities and people and through maintaining a higher state we can start to experience a deepening sense of engagement with our work, which in turn becomes far more rewarding.

Within this section we will explore the implications of our state. Together we will cover what is going on when we embody differing energetic states. We will look at how lower states can create the perception of stress in the workplace, along with the steps we might take to maintain higher states. With those higher states we will also look at the possibilities through the attaining of FLOW states, the experiencing of harmony between you and the work you are engaged in.

So what is your state at this precise moment?

Do you have an awareness of your state from moment to moment? In the sales environment there can be a rather broad array of energies exhibited by salespeople. For the salesperson on a roll, high energy can be experienced and felt by others around them, a positivity in the way they engage with people and an enthusiasm for the job. Contrastingly, those in a lower state, maybe due to a lost deal, a missed opportunity or being daunted by the prospect of the quarter end, things are tedious. They might find things to be difficult, that it is hard to be positive about events and circumstances in the situation they think they are in. Often accompanying the lower state can be an internal dialogue running, commentating on their situation. This mental dialogue might call into question the worth of their activity or complain that they don't want to be doing whatever it is they are engaged in, and wish to be elsewhere. That mental noise is self-fulfilling and further draining of what we might describe as psychic energy, which in turn can keep the person in a low state.

It is quite common for salespeople to harbour underlying feelings of mild resentment towards certain functions of their job from time to time. It was something I encountered during my career. There are always elements to the job we enjoy less than others. For me it was making outbound cold calls to prospective companies, however during the outward expansion of my career as a new business hunter it was a large part of what was expected from me. I went through cycles of flowing with the calling sessions and then periods of resentment towards them. That resentment was often a result of not getting my desired outcomes from the time spent calling, that is to say, not booking any appointments.

As my career developed, moving from one role to the next I experienced the conflict between what I was actually good at doing, finding new business (which at that time was largely a telephone-based activity) and the feeling that I didn't want to chase after new business anymore. Meaning that in my mind at that time I felt as if I had done enough cold calling, because back then I did not really enjoy it all that much. So periodically, typically after an unproductive calling session, I would encounter resistance and resentment manifesting as the thought that I did not want to be doing that aspect of the job anymore and on occasions I would question whether sales was something I wanted to continue with. Those feelings were largely consequential to frustration and disappointment rather than how I actually felt about my career path as a whole; thus when those thoughts shifted and my equilibrium restored, the thoughts and feelings encountered quickly evaporated.

Others I have worked with over the years have also remarked on occasionally encountering feelings of frustration associated with tasks like capturing details of poor quality meetings they had recently attended. Some complained about recording call details or updating opportunities in the CRM, or perhaps managing an account list full of poor quality accounts that demanded too much attention whilst having little perceived value. Whatever it was, those feelings were negative thoughts towards what they were engaged in.

These feelings may not be your prevailing feelings but from time to time they are there and it can become a bit of a broken record. If you can relate to those feelings of frustration or irritation towards any aspects of your job, can you truly say you are fully productive at that time, if in some part your energy is being consumed by the feeling of resentment?

So how does the supposedly energetic, motivated, enthusiastic salesperson we advertise ourselves to be in the job interview snap out of that feeling, that mind-state? If we find ourselves in that state, is it something that we are able to purposefully change? Does it just work itself out, maybe in a few minutes, hours, or worse, does it take much longer to shift? Do you even realise you have dropped into a lower state? The good news is yes, we can change it if we see it happening or better still we can take steps to strengthen our higher states to avoid the drop altogether.

Your state, whatever that may be in any given moment, is something that emanates from within, but depending on the individual it can be affected to varying degrees by external situations or events. Everyone emanates an encompassing and surrounding field of energy that corresponds to their inner state. Most people have experienced it.

Although when they do they may feel someone else's energy (state), only subliminally, so that they don't know that they sense it, yet it determines to a large extent how they feel about and how they react to that person. Some people are most clearly aware of energetic state when they first meet someone and even before any words are exchanged it helps define the first impression they form around someone.

Having a higher state versus a lower state is apparent to people you come into contact with. The better you know the person the more likely you will be to sense their emotional and energetic state, especially when you ask how they are doing and their response seems to be counter to what you pick up energetically.

Now, ask yourself, do you know people that exhibit high or low states? Someone who sees the glass as half empty, rather than half full? Maybe in the sales meeting they are the person that always has a reason why the deal never came in. To those individuals it would seem that bad luck just seems to happen to them. Do you ever sense an undercurrent of negativity about them or their attitude to the activity they are undertaking at any given moment? I ask because that could never be you, right? It has been my experience in every company I have worked in that there is always someone with high energy, not uncommonly the high performer in the team, with their counterpart at the lower end of the energetic scale, and whilst it is fair to say some of the low-energy type did well at meeting their targets each month, it was always with gritted teeth and an accompanying story of what was unfair, difficult or why it wasn't better. What has been your experience of being amongst people with high or lower energy? On balance did you feel better or worse from time spent with them? Maybe you see your own reflection in this?

Let us now explore the nature of state, the way in which it can influence the experience of events as they unfold around you, and look at why you might see things as stressful or unlucky. We will look at the idea of luck and being unlucky and then explore the practices which can raise your state, pulling from both traditional and emerging techniques.

Chapter 6 – The Nature of State

Your state can influence the way you interact with and relate to events of everyday life. For the purposes of further illustrating how state plays out on what we see and how we respond I would like to introduce you to John, a senior account manager at a fictitious technology company. John is really an amalgamation of the many salespeople I have worked with over the years, brought to life here to shine a light on how the hidden workings of our minds can influence the world as we see it and the steps we might take to optimise our impact on the world at large.

John thinks himself reasonably successful, managing a small group of large accounts. For the most part John enjoys his job, but he gets bogged down with the notion that from time to time he has bad luck. He is married with a new baby, and like most young infants the baby can and does frequently cry at night. Like other growing families, money can be short from time to time and for John it adds to the underlying sense of pressure he feels to meet his sales targets, to provide for his family. This particular morning John awakens having slept badly; in fact he hardly slept at all for the teething new baby kept the family awake all night with her crying. In his mind John starts playing out a little self-pity dialogue. From time to time maybe you have also heard something similar? "Oh why today? I need sleep; why did I have to be kept awake last night. What a great start to the day!"

That voice in your head, sometimes fleeting, is at other times always there to add commentary to the situation. Very rarely does it add any value to your day or your sense of wellbeing, and most of all it is always uninvited. It just starts talking.

Over breakfast he opens the morning post and is further deflated when he receives an unexpected bill. Immediately his thoughts and the internal running dialogue turn to "That's just great, another bill, just my luck. One more thing to find the money for", and "Why does this happen now, today of all days? I could do without this meeting first thing".

Of course this all plays out in the privacy of his head. He finishes his breakfast, kisses his wife and baby goodbye and leaves the house to travel to his meeting.

It is an important first meeting with a new main contact within one of his larger accounts. There is already some apprehension in John's mind towards the meeting; he has learnt from speaking with other people from within the account that the new VP for Technology is a really tough customer and can be very demanding. John, already a few minutes late leaving the house, makes his way to the meeting by car and is frustrated when he encounters heavy traffic that could make him late, further adding stress to his already affected state.

How do you think the events of his morning will affect how he comes across during the meeting? Would it affect you and the way you are received?

Well, it may be stating the obvious but things happen, and depending on what those events are and the degree to which you let those events affect you, ultimately they can influence your state negatively. It means your change of state can impact upon how you see the events unfolding around you. When it comes to those changes in your state, your underlying sense of wellbeing, do you think others can or will pick up on that change? If you can sense it in others can you really hide it in yourself?

As with our example, what might John's state be as he goes into his meeting? Is he likely to be stress-free and positive, fully focused on creating a good first impression with the new VP? Even if he has put it out of his mind as he walks through his client's door, it is very probable that at some subconscious level he will still be carrying the negative emotion of his perceived bad luck, the traffic that made him late, the unexpected bill or the feeling that he's not had enough sleep. If minor or major frustrations are encountered, not letting go of them quickly as they arise will result in them being carried around with you. This means a certain amount of your energetic resources are going to be consumed in dealing with the containment of that frustration along with the processing of the potential consequences your mind starts to quantify, which is simply your resistance to the events that played out.

What has been your experience? Do you overcome the bumps in the road easily or do they get picked up and carried around inside you? Do you ever find yourself doing one thing at work, trying to focus your concentration on a particular task but maybe unable to remain focused? Realising that a part of your mind is wrestling with a past event or problem, one that seems unwilling to go away, something to which your mind keeps returning?

Your state, the energy you embody, is a dynamic thing. It changes from moment to moment, and it can be changed positively from one moment to the next by you simply choosing to let go of the external things that gave rise to the frustration: the unexpected bill, the traffic, or whatever it was that "happened". You cannot change the external world once it has happened, but you can change the way you choose to react to it. I am pretty sure that most people, if not everyone, has come across this notion, whether it was said to them in a difficult moment, they read it somewhere or experienced it in some other way. How many of you have stopped and considered the implications of the idea? How many have given any real consideration as to how it might actually improve the experience of their career or at a wider level the impact it would have on their life? The extent to which you allow external events to influence you, and in what way, is actually down to you.

People can and do pick up on these shifts in state, noticeable more commonly in people we know. Typically and maybe wrongly these changes in state are casually labelled as moods, and moods can be good or bad. Have you given thought to what the impact of a low state is to those around you? If, like our account manager John, your first appointment of the day is with a new contact, or maybe a call with your largest client, and you're in an off mood, how do you think the energy you project and which the new client experiences will shape his first impression of you? Does the way in which your voice carries the words of your call shape the way you are heard by your largest account? These subtleties will at some level reflect the state you are in and be projected outwards.

The impact of your state could be as simple or as subtle as a change in your normal body language, perhaps a little less relaxed, not in your normal flow, or the way that your voice changes with pitch and tone whilst speaking. It could be that your tolerance to minor frustrations is lowered and that may be picked up on. If all these subtleties are possible, could they really affect the outcome?

It becomes especially interesting when you consider that the premise of what we do as sales professionals is around the efficacy of our communication. We can measure the impact on our clients as a correlation between the strength of our message and their acceptance of it. The closer the key points of the message align with the ideas, beliefs and needs of the client, the more impactful and influential the exchange becomes and the more strongly our value proposition is delivered. So presenting an idea positively, with corresponding energy, tonality and enthusiasm always plays a part in the way in which the client interprets and analyses what we say even if they are not consciously aware of it.

For John, our troubled account manager, he arrived a few minutes late which in his mind set the meeting off to a bad start. The meeting lasted around an hour and covered off the main points that both John and the VP wanted to discuss. Moreover, whilst nothing was said to suggest the meeting had not been successful, John left feeling deflated, that it did not go as well as it might have, and that he was not on his best game. The big sales opportunity of a technology refresh that John wanted to explore with the customer did get discussed, however not as deeply or with strong follow-up actions as John would have liked.

Learning not to label events

What could our deflated account manager John have done differently? Alternatively, how might the meeting have gone if John was completely detached from the preceding events and operating at a positive, that is higher, state? Well, the simple answer is we do not know, it is an example, but the truth is to be discovered by you in the practice of detachment from labelling so-called bad events. It is a letting go of the compulsive continuous labelling of things which our minds attempt to make sense of, to measure their meaning and pretty much always against our past experiences. In those instances when the event or occurrence isn't consistent with our desired outcome, that is to say what we want to happen, it becomes something the voice in the head, the ego, can argue and wrestle with, complaining in some way, something that most if not all of us experience from time to time.

By being aware of the greater potentialities of each and every situation that you might have quickly labelled negatively, as the example depicts, as "bad luck happening" to you, you start to free yourself from the limited perspective of the complaining voice in your head. Change starts at ground zero, and that means change is achieved through the awareness of yourself, and monitoring your thoughts and energy. Maintaining a higher state is possible and we will explore some of the practices to achieve this later in the chapter.

From here on in I want you to approach this material experientially, by which I mean I want you to start practising the approaches as they are shared, which means starting here with the practising of non-judgement, the non-labelling of events and situations to see what may arise from the highest state you can hold. This approach must be practised consistently; you must give any situation or event time to unfold as to its true meaning. This means that the real significance of an event does not always become clear immediately. Frequently it takes time to pass for events to fall into a place where greater meaning can be derived from them, and even then that greater meaning doesn't necessarily resolve to a good or bad judgement. It just means that there is a discernible pattern from the events that resulted in you being where you are in that precise moment.

What this practice reveals is that all events and situations that might have been at one time labelled as bad were simply events and situations amongst the continuous flow of situations and events. If the so-called bad ones did not happen, can it be said with any certainty that any of us would be where we are in this moment; would different experiences have taken us down different paths? Everything that happened has brought us to where we are. Personally, I am happy with where I am, and if that is true then the events that brought me here were all part of a necessary process. It became apparent to me that to judge specific aspects of my journey, or to wish them otherwise, even if at the time they were unhelpful, difficult or unpleasant, in retrospect was rather pointless since those events were all part of what ultimately led me to this moment.

Allowing time to pass without judgement will most likely be a challenge to you, as the egoic voice in your head will want to pigeonhole the situation and make sense of things according to its interpretation of reality. Is it not fair to say that the compulsive aspect of you, the voice in your head, frequently offers up thoughts and criticisms without invitation, casting an opinion of what is what in relation to what might be unfolding in that moment or reflecting on what has already taken place? It is easy to identify with the voice, those continuous thoughts as to who you really are; it is entirely natural. It has always been there and gives you a very real sense of who you are, allowing you to rationalise, intellectualise, and make judgements about your place in the world, but it is not you. It's a facet, a part of your resources and most likely completely out of balance with your sense of wellbeing.

If you are going to practise just letting things be as they are without judgement you must have some faith, belief or just plain old discipline: a desire to improve upon your current experience at the very least. Whatever you believe in, whether a higher order of things or feeling that there can be more to an event than your immediate take on it, you will benefit from the practice of non-judgement, of not labelling. In Part 4 we will explore in greater detail the importance of belief and where it fits in on the path to achieving your desired successful outcomes.

The nature and role of luck

Does our sense of being lucky affect our state? Do we feel better when the stars are aligned and it seems everything is going our way? What is luck anyway? Is it random or is it as an old manager of mine once said, "I am a great believer in luck. The harder I work, the more of it I seem to have", which could be read as you make your own luck. This is closer to my own feelings about the idea of luck. That it is the way you look at things and the beliefs about them that appear to influence your experience of luck. Like the saying goes, "If you think you're lucky or you think you're unlucky you're probably right."

So how can you influence luck so that it is the good variety? Is it actually influence, or some kind of attraction? Could it be we actually draw things to us including outcomes, often described as luck, whether they are good or bad? Perhaps success, for that matter, and what would it mean if those outcomes were directly linked to our state? If that were possible it would probably make a big difference to the way we approach opportunities and maybe take a lot of the anxiety out of the sales situations that can arise to challenge us day to day.

The trouble with luck is that it isn't very scientific. It's not quantifiable, and by its common meaning it's not repeatable. It's a rather emotive concept; to some it's the means of explaining why a deal never closed or to others it was the added nudge that got the contract signed. When we speak of luck or chance what is meant varies depending upon the person perceiving the event. The kind of upbringing they have had plays a major role, such as their religious or cultural background, or even the emotional context of the one interpreting it.

To many in the western world luck is seen as a purposeless, unpredictable and uncontrollable force that shapes events favourably or unfavourably, according to the observer, events that influence one's life and are seemingly beyond one's control. On the whole people experience luck and life for that matter as something that is happening to them, and that luck, good or bad, happens regardless of the individual. However what if your luck or success changed according to your energetic state?

For the purpose of this discourse, as we speak of luck let's recontextualise the meaning for the moment. Rather than it being viewed as random events inflicted upon us, try to see the notion of luck not as random chance, but as one of super potentiality. By this I mean the experiencing of an event where there might be multiple outcomes possible at any given time, rather than being limited to the one immediately perceived by the individual.

The notion of super potentiality would mean that the state at which we operate directly corresponds to the forces at work, and importantly changes the filter through which the experiencing individual perceives the event. When things happen to us we often use labels to categorise the value of the event, such as good or bad. It helps us define its meaning, and is often done very quickly, automatically in fact. The event or occurrence is filtered through a mental lens, so that subconsciously we ask if the immediate situation serves or hinders us. The value judgement is further compounded, as the pattern recognition aspect of the brain will be sorting for previous or similar instances of this outcome to substantiate the prevailing value judgement.

Once we have defined the event or situation as being bad, we lose or seriously impair our opportunity to see it as something else. Our mind continues to look for evidence to validate the "bad" judgement we have made and any other potential outcomes that might have been experienced are missed.

This is unconscious behaviour and was put thus by Amos Tversky, a cognitive and mathematical psychologist, when showing how in our personal and professional lives things happen that are confusing or appear a mystery when initially encountered. However from the midst of that uncertainty the individual would soon arrive at an explanation or theory to make sense from the facts so as to make them fit with their version of how things happen and why:

"In contrast to our skill in inventing scenarios, explanations, and interpretations, our ability to access their likelihood, or to evaluate them critically, is grossly inadequate. Once we have adopted a particular hypothesis or interpretation, we grossly exaggerate the likelihood of that hypothesis, and find it very difficult to see things any other way."[5]

Simply put, we have an unconscious habit of trying to explain through invention the reasons behind and the significance of unfolding events that do not fit into our desired view of the world. Those inventions are constructed from within the cache of our past experiences and depending on your state will either have a positive or negative slant, because that is how you will have interpreted the events.

Try to look at the event dispassionately and not judge it immediately. If you can change the way you look at things, the things you look at will start to change. This becomes easier as you consistently maintain a higher state. Little things – those bumps in the road – do not register as problems so easily any longer. By not labelling everything that would quite normally have been put down to chance as either being "good or bad" there exists space for a different interpretation. I am not suggesting that you start to look upon what you consider as "good" events differently, but do not let those normally labelled as "bad" cloud the way you experience the event.

The real outcome may yet be revealed as opportune. This is of course easier said than done, but if you allow the idea of super potentiality to be there, and accept that there is the possibility of opportunity in every situation and event, then immediately you have stepped into a new paradigm of potential. From that place you will no longer be limited by the idea of good or bad luck imposed upon you by a cruel world of chance or kept prisoner as to what something means by the past programming of your mind.

---

[5] Michael Lewis, 2016, *The Undoing Project*, W.W. Norton & Company, pp. 205–206.

Some might reasonably think that each day, in the undertaking of our duties, certain "events" just seem to come along to get in our way. Think about it for a moment. If those events and people, for that matter, obstruct you from achieving, reaching and succeeding in what you set out to do if you're a high energy individual, or if you're not high energy then to you those events slow you, drag you down, drain your energy, then maybe the next few minutes reading this will start the process of recontextualising your experiences.

To start with I would like to go a little abstract on how we see things and how they might actually be. Most people relate to life as something you move through: you get born, you start growing and all this stuff happens as you progress through your experiences. Ok? Agreed? Such as "On the way to work this happened to me", or "We want to go on holiday but don't have the time or money".

We have this belief that we are moving through life as if to arrive somewhere, the next job, a new home, a better position of financial security, then on to where? Ultimately to our coffins, but is that really what is happening? Are we really moving through the experience of life as if on some animated journey or are we actually looking at it the wrong way and it is that we are actually not moving and the experiences we call forth are coming up to meet our expectations, intentions and beliefs?

Can I offer a possible explanation? Think about it for a moment; are we all just fixed points and it is the reality we create that is dynamic? Ok, so what, who cares, does it change anything? And the answer I feel to be true is yes, that it matters, it changes everything.

You may experience walking to work, finishing a task, climbing a mountain but... these are just interpretations, electrical impulses from our sensory organs, touch, sight, sound, smell taste, etcetera; they are not actually real in the knowable sense. This is not a new idea. We know that how we actually perceive the world is through those electrical impulses being processed in the brain from which a structured image of the world is rendered. This has been and will continue to be explored and debated for a long time to come, but if we just accept this as the experiential functioning of our senses and of our environment could it be argued that we aren't really here at all and in fact you are plugged into the most complex neuro-interactive simulation ever?

Sound familiar? Well of course, the popular science fiction movie *The Matrix* pointed to such a reality, albeit with a dystopian slant. Still not sure? Ok, we have created a microcosmic, albeit limited, version of this idea in the realm of the Internet and the collaboration with virtual reality, and the more recently and more widely accepted and adopted augmented reality. In VR the user puts on a headset, and depending on the sophistication of the interactive instruments, also items ranging from VR gloves to full immersion bodysuits that can simulate all manner of experiences without the user actually leaving the relative confines of the VR space they occupy.

So how does the previous idea sound now? Are we moving through life or are the experiences being called forth and played out/lived out as it is without any real awareness that the experiences are all pre-programmed?

Let me just expand on that for a moment. I just said that all your experiences are pre-programmed, or framed differently, prepared for you in advance. This of course will rattle some, annoy others and for the majority of the people that this finds its way to will be completely rejected out of hand. Why? What is so abhorrent?

"I don't like the idea that I don't have choice."

"Life is freedom of choice and what you're suggesting is that it is pre-ordained, that I am destined to follow a set of events."

"We all have free will to determine our paths."

"I just don't believe in any of this new age thought."

And the list of rejections goes on. But, and it's a big one, what if the previous proposition was slightly adjusted by you, the reader, to allow you to understand a slightly wider, deeper, broader sense of its meaning?

What if the implication that everything is prepared for you was expanded so that you realise the meaning is not that the prepared events are limited to those that you are experiencing and have experienced, but are simply the ones that you have called fourth unconsciously?

What if the entire spectrum of possible outcomes was all just waiting for you to bring forth, to experience the ones you choose? I use the word "choose" very loosely as for most people it is not choosing but a series of consequential experiences.

And let's frame that totality of prepared experiences as what I have come to describe as super potentiality, that every, that is EVERY, possible outcome is potentially available to the experiencer. Much in the same way a modern video game works where you adopt the role of the main protagonist and explore the virtual game environment, interacting with others and experiencing all the functions of the game with the experiential understanding that you have a free will to move and act as you choose within the relative confines of the game, which for certain games that mirror aspects of human existence applies the same laws of physics e.g. you jump but gravity brings you down to earth.

If you think about it, that game, the structure and architecture of which has been built for you to operate within, must have programming for every possible movement and interaction scenario. If you go left and hit a wall the game will reflect that. Turn right and see another game player, the image is seamlessly rendered and the consequential outcomes of that move are potentially ready to be called forth. Each and every move is pre-programmed and waiting to be accessed through the game player's decision, or shall we say intention, to do something.

So is the game player really moving or is a sequence of events being brought to the conscious awareness of the player in order to sequentialise a set of unifying experiences rendered on screen and then in the player's mind to create a virtual reality in which the player is immersed? If anyone knows avid gamers, it is pretty real to them. So what are the actual differences between the game architecture and what I have posited as to the nature of your life experience?

The universe is one giant immeasurable interaction of super potentiality that anything and everything is there waiting to be called forth. It really is a game experience.

Now, I will generalise a little here but it's fair to say that most men don't read instructions, and it might be a stretch but I will venture further and say that in the world of gameplay people don't read the user guide, in favour of just getting stuck in. Now doesn't that also sound a little familiar; how many people given the global population of, say, 7 billion, have considered that there might be a set of instructions to navigating life and of those few, how many have actually read them? We might call those user manuals holy texts: the Bible, Koran, and Torah etc. Not everyone's preferred reading or necessarily spot on with their instruction, given the opportunity for distortion and misunderstanding along the way by those seeking to promote the message or themselves as knowers of the message.

But what the vast majority of people do is work it out as they go along. Of course as in the game play there are other players that offer hints and tips, some of which are valuable. Others, however, well let's just say they are at best well-intentioned but miss the mark.

So how many of you are still with me? Well, it's of no great importance because it's not that serious, since it is, as I BELIEVE, a game, and even though at the time of playing, gamers take the game play seriously, at the end of the experience they know if they die on level 3 they just start over and do it again, and keep playing, searching for ways to overcome whatever stopped them in the last game they played.

"Ah, but that's because it's not real. There is no real consequence of them crashing out on level 3 or level 30 for that matter, it's not as if they die in real life" – to which I say "and...?"

What's the difference in the game we call life? What distinguishes the reality of the game from the reality of your life experience? I want to separate the expression "your life" from "your life experience". You are intricately woven into the fabric of reality, that reality we call existence, and on a personal level we call life, but actually we are LIFE and we have life experiences.

And so, back to the question, how do the two scenarios actually differ?

Well of course it's a glib question. We all believe we know the answer to the question, in that the existence feels real: it has painful or joyous consequences. But I take you back to the beginning of this discourse and remind you that experientially it is all just a set of electrical impulses interpreted in the mind. We know this because of the work carried out in the field of neuroscience.

Now let's imagine that we had the minds of a goldfish, popularly considered as having a very short memory. Imagine that everything you experienced was quite literally experienced and then let go of, or forgotten. It is because of that lack of memory that everything experienced would be almost if not entirely a brand new experience without any prior ideas, experiences or beliefs about it, and therefore nothing to contextually frame the event in the present moment.

How would that affect the way you handled situations? Do you think that would lead to positive, liberating outcomes as you are not attached to ideas from the past, which link your thinking to old paradigms? It could be viewed both ways: as a disaster or an entirely liberating experience.

The experiencing of life without emotional attachment is not the case for pretty much the entire planet. What everyone does including me (I am in the same game as you lot), is that we collect experiences and we use those experiences to frame our understanding of whatever it is that appears before us. And it goes even further than just framing the context; it also can and frequently does distort the reality, that is to say the events as they are rather than as we interpret them. It is in our interpretation that the distortion takes place. We see things as we THINK they are rather than how they actually are. This is why a group of people can witness the same event and recount different experiences and identify with different aspects of the event.

Right, anyone want to leave the game yet? No? Good, because this is where it gets interesting. What if you not only realised that this was the nature of life; what if you recognised the events as being moments in a game and that more importantly you had read the instructions on how to play?

Imagine the whole of your personal universe, the entirety of your experiences, as a giant planet-sized spherical flicker book with every possible outcome that you could ever imagine and that someone explained how you could choose which moment came next, and the one after that and the one after that. A giant spinning ball of potential moments moving so fast as to seem seamless.

And what if that understanding, when practised daily, aligned you, put you in harmony with the organising principles of each and every other being's experiences in the universe such that a synchronicity started to become abundantly apparent and unified those beings' experiences into a singular harmonious sequence of events? What would that mean for your life and your attitudes towards it?

So where are the instructions? Well actually it might surprise you or it might not, given that you are all reading this, that each of us have them inside. Every single one of us has the means within ourselves to synchronise with the reality of our choosing but have allowed those instructions to become clouded over by years of experiential conditioning to the contrary of the true nature of things.

Put simply, we have programmed ourselves and society to believe that life is a particular way and despite the continuous and endless ways in which the organising principles of the universe may offer themselves to each and every one of you, we find our self disconnected from the resourcefulness to access this universal resource.

So, as Lao Tzu wrote centuries ago, every journey starts with a single step. That step is to understand that you are the creator of your experiences, you are the one controlling the game, and not, as the world might lead us to believe, that the world controls our experiences.

That awakening, realisation, whatever labels works best for you, will take you to the next step. And you need only remember this: that in every journey, in every endeavour, you need only take one step at a time.

If, like Alice, you want to see what is down the rabbit hole, then the next step is to recognise that your life force, your energy, your STATE, is the primary point to be aware of. When you realise that energy is magnetic and each of us has emanating from within a bioelectrical energy field that extends beyond physical boundaries and allows us to interact with our environment and others at a higher level, imperceptible to most, then you start to appreciate that the energy we vibrate at, the energetic state we operate with, largely determines the kind of people we connect with and events that we encounter.

And because at this awareness stage you are simply now awake to the realisation but not actively driving the game, you can see that each and every person you interact with has a similar if not the same corresponding energetic state. If we then arrange those energetic states into an organised and quantifiable structure for which we have Dr David Hawkins to thank for his work in bringing that awareness to the fore, then we can see how the organising principles of the universe arrange each being's experience in accordance to the energetic state they operate at. Try not to get hung up on the expression "organising principles of the universe"; you can call it life if that is easier for you to accept.

So don't look at the possible outcomes as simply one globelike flicker sphere in a series of parallel spheres representing everyone else. In framing the experience we are not only horizontally arranged, in that along the horizontal plane you resonate with like-minded souls, but open your mind to the possibility that hierarchically there are different strata of these super potentialities – these flicker spheres or possible moments and outcomes – organised and structured depending on the energy vibration from a log scale of 20 to 1000, as described in Hawkins' *Power vs. Force*.[6]

That is why we attract like-minded souls; we don't perceive certain situations to be the same as another because the vibrational state in which we operate impacts the way in which we perceive and process the events. Which means that what one person labels as bad luck contextually defined by their filters (or life experiences and governed by their vibrational state) another person at a higher energetic state, one who overcomes the need to label, to rationalise and have it fit into a smaller scale model that they can hold in their minds, sees the same event as an opportunity or at least remains neutral as to the meaning until such time that the true nature becomes clearer.

So it simply means that the higher our energetic state the more capable we are of taking in our stride the ripples and bumps in the road that the life experience conjures. Now, do not think for a moment that those higher energetic state beings don't encounter challenges. Of course they experience what others might label as problems, but from a higher vantage point the issue doesn't seem that big. Or they perceive the greater meaning behind the events and as such have at their disposal the entirety or at least a higher degree of their resourcefulness to direct towards addressing the event. In short they stop making things into problems and just deal with the bumps in the road as if that's all they are, just bumps, not problems.

---

[6] David R. Hawkins M.D., Ph.D, 2012, *Power vs. Force*, Hay House Inc, appendices B & C, p. 308.

So we must practise raising our state. We all know intuitively what lifts our spirits: things like listening to music, meditation, dancing, and exercise, but state changing is not limited to these activities. There are many ways to raise state; you are the best judge for yourself. These are just suggested as they have shown consistency in the results they yield. All these practised regularly enable the raising of one's vibrational state. Practise these approaches for a month or longer and notice within yourself the differences. Whether that means you are calmer, or that you have more vitality or simply don't get stressed over the things that used to get you down, you are ready to continue to the phase of accessing life moments and experiences, those that you wish to experience, and you will in effect start being a player of the game rather than the one being played.

Chapter Summary

The Nature of State

- Your state is the primary point to be aware of.
- Pay attention to changes in your state, noticing what triggers the change.
- Present ideas positively, with corresponding energy, tonality and enthusiasm. You never know the impact you might have on someone.
- Make awareness of your thoughts and where your mind wanders to part of your daily practice.
- It's a game; be the player and not the played.

Chapter 7 – Life is a Canvas

If we accept that the idea of super potentiality reflects greater and numerous possible outcomes, and that when we speak of super potentiality from an individual perspective it reflects the potential outcomes beyond those which are immediately apparent through the filter of one's past experiences, we can see that in any given moment we have the choice to see something as one thing or another and depending upon our energetic state it has an effect on the range of possible outcomes we may be potentially aware of.

The higher your state, the less inhibiting and potentially the more opportune the outcome may be perceived, but not necessarily. Each and every moment, therefore every event or situation in our lives, is connected to everything else in the world in an infinitely complex web of interacting events. Nothing really happens that does not have an influence upon something else, yet it may not always be visibly evident. Life is not experienced in a vacuum. What we are exploring here is the relationship between state and your inner sense of wellbeing in relation to the events of the world as they unfold.

Not everyone is ready to hear that idea, that nothing is ever separate, that everything is fundamentally interconnected with everything else. I know a lot of people struggle to accept the idea that everything is connected in some way but try to reconcile yourself with this idea. Consider a world famous painting, let's say the Mona Lisa, which is recognisable to most people in the western world. Firstly let's say you were looking down on the painting, but you did not know it was the Mona Lisa because you were only able to focus upon a tiny part, a single square centimetre of the painting. If that single square centimetre was all you could see, what you were looking at would most likely be incomprehensible and unidentifiable. To the observer it would be just a small random blob of colour or colours merging together without any meaning. It would be virtually impossible to identify from which larger picture it was a part and certainly difficult if not impossible to judge the value of that painting from such a limited perspective. Even if you were given a succession of single squares to look upon, each would only offer the same tiny fractured perspective. It is possible some people might start to draw comparisons between the squares, giving those distinctions a value judgement, seeing the light colours as better or preferable to the darker ones but ultimately the observer would still not be able to appreciate the entirety of the work.

Can you see how your life experiences, from the perspective of making judgements about things you encounter, about them being good or bad, could be seen as those squares of colour?

Your present moment awareness could be looked upon in the same way, as a tiny piece of the whole picture. The present moment is that tiny square of colour, sometimes light, sometimes dark, but for many people quite indistinguishable as to the significance against the whole of which it is part. If that were all we were to say about it that would be fine, but accompanying the interaction with each of those squares, those present moments that seamlessly merge into a continuous experience, is the burden of meaning which we add to those colourful squares, the judgement that the lighter moments are the good ones but the darker ones, well, do we keep a count of the dark moments? Ever ready to add them to the growing list, reinforcing the idea, which over time becomes a belief, that the dark squares, those difficult moments, are in some way bad and undesirable.

Because that's all there is from your perspective: just your interpretation of the present moment, a tiny square of colour most likely filtered through the lens of your past experiences. All those other squares you've encountered and judged as to the meaning.

Now what happens when the entirety of the picture is revealed to you? Your perspective, your comprehension of all those little squares immediately changes. You no longer focus on the square but perceive the image as a whole, and suddenly all of those dark squares that did not appear to mean so much suddenly create the contrast necessary for your appreciation of the whole of the painting.

This changing of perspective brings context to the original single centimetre. As the image becomes revealed, what started off as a meaningless blob of colour starts to reveal itself as part of a masterpiece.

They say art imitates life, which I think is pretty apt given that your life experience, your present moment awareness, is much like the tiny blob of colour on Da Vinci's canvas. Regardless of how meaningless or unpleasant that present moment may feel, if you can hold in mind that the moment is part of something much bigger, a grand masterpiece much like Da Vinci's, it may become easier to accept that not understanding the event you are experiencing is not to suggest it isn't part of the perfection that is your life. If you can do that then you have moved closer into harmony with the organising principles of the universe, allowing the super potentiality, the dynamic possibilities of the universe, to bring forward to you the experience that best serves your growth in all that you do in the workplace and indeed in your wider experience of life.

It is true that from a higher state perspective you don't notice, that is you do not naturally lean towards, the possible negative interpretations of a given moment. If you hold a higher state you have most likely let go of some thoughts and beliefs about why things happen. It is when we are tuned to a higher frequency that we are tuned to the interpretation and perception of higher potential outcomes whereas by contrast when we occupy a lower state we align our perception with lower, negative outcomes.

It is important to make clear that from ANY state we find ourselves in, ultimately we have the choice to choose the significance and meaning of the events that unfold around us and not unconsciously process the experience through the lens of the past. Nevertheless, to do this one must be present. We must be vigilant to our thoughts and where our attention is in any given moment. If this sounds like exhausting work, to the initiate it will undoubtedly feel as such. I remind you as described within this book that what I speak of has to be practised. This is not something to be tried once and put away like an interesting book. It is to be picked up daily. It is to be incorporated into your working day.

So why am I telling you all this? I think the meaning behind the painting analogy is self-evident. We cannot always know what is ultimately going to lead us to "where we want to be" and this discernment can be made easier, or the moment less conflictory from a higher state, but the key point here, the thing I want you to stop and consider now for a few moments, is that it doesn't matter what your state is. What is important to remember is you always have a choice as to how you respond to what is going on around you. It is very easy to forget you have that choice when you live your life from within your head. When you view the events dispassionately, for what they actually are rather than what you think they mean, you create a little space.

You can find that space by asking yourself "Am I present?" In the asking you become so. You start to experience space between your thoughts and related judgements of what is happening and you become the witness to those thoughts and judgements. From there you may find it possible to accept the event without judging. When you occupy that space you tap into great strength. You have the capacity to choose your response, even if the event's "meanings" aren't immediately apparent, which things seldom are. You determine how you respond and what version of yourself you show to the world in response to what is happening. Even when you don't know the meaning or the reason, something happens and you can find peace in the knowledge that you are experiencing a tiny fragment of an immense canvas.

How is it that the same event can be viewed by different people who all take away from it a different perspective or potential outcome?

Example

Take an example, let's say John our account manager again. He one day buys a lottery ticket and wins an expensive car, but after driving the car around for a few days John is involved in a traffic accident when a drunk driver crashes into him at a junction. John is injured and ends up in hospital. One night whilst his family is visiting him in the hospital there is a fire at his house and it burns to the ground.

At each stage of this story it is easy to quickly assign a value label against each situation. Broken down we might typically judge accordingly:

John wins a car – seen as good luck

John has a bad accident in car – looked upon as bad luck; had he not won the car he would not have been crashed into and thus not ended up in hospital.

John's home burns to the ground – perceived as bad luck? It could be viewed as either good or bad, could it not? Bad that he has lost his home, however we cannot escape the fact that had he not been in the hospital he and his family would most likely have perished in the fire. The facts are the facts; they do not change. What can change is the value and meaning placed on each. The degree to which an individual perspective can change positively is reflected by their awareness of the impact state has.

This little story seeks to illustrate how easy it is to label a situation; it is automatic in fact to label and therefore define an event, reducing the super potentiality of the situation. It's not dissimilar to saying, "I know it", which reduces the possibility for greater understanding at a conscious level. By labelling the event you have judged it, defined it and decided what it means, and in deciding that meaning you are significantly limiting your awareness to other potentialities.

The stress and strain of the job

A career in sales is not for everyone; for those of us who've chosen this career path we all know it to be the greatest job and the worst. Depending on your perspective, the stress or strain we experience is ongoing without end. We continuously pursue a target monthly, quarterly or annually. I recall a conversation once where a manager at that time explained how he had stopped looking at his career in respect of years as a sales professional but simply how many months and years of targets he had met successfully.

A sales career is quite different to most others and eventually starts to change the way you frame your perception; it certainly has mine. You start to examine things more closely as to their meaning and the likelihood of a given outcome, both in the job and outside in the wider sense. Sales often encourage the individual to ask more questions of the situation. This qualification is important in a sales situation, as we all know, but it is also important to place our own state of being underneath the lens of that examination and frequently, doing so allows for awareness of where we are coming from in the formation of ideas and opinions. If we are not aware of our state from which we make evaluations, conclusions and decisions we lose objectivity as to the quality of those undertakings, as in those situations we are more likely to be reacting to events based not only on our past experiences, but our state affecting the interpretation, not consciously responding to whatever is unfolding. This is done potentially in a repetitive mode of thinking, falling into patterns of prediction through our proficiency of doing these tasks every day with thought processes becoming automatic, as described in Chapter 3 when discussing how proficiency and experience can put us in danger of losing some of our objectivity.

In order to thrive in a challenging and competitive sales environment you must have self-awareness, remaining flexible and fluid in your actions and thoughts, responding to a continuously changing landscape. Whether that is in response to changes in competition or the adjustment the overall organisation makes to stay relevant and competitive, for every change that takes place you, the sales professional, must respond consciously to accommodate the change. Failing to do so consistently is to become rigid and if nature is any indicator, it is the old oak that topples whilst the flexible sapling moves with the wind.

What we might deem stressful at work is actually an interpretation of strain, something we all encounter in the carrying out of our duties day to day. The difference is that the strain becomes stress when we become ill equipped to deal with it, when we lose the balance between challenge and ability, especially noticeable in the work environment. This is likely to be due to additional external factors exerting an influence on you at a time you are overwhelmed or managing a multitude of things in your work situation, which given another day, another time, you might have shrugged off quickly and moved on.

Many salespeople have described the job as being incredibly stressful, but is that really an accurate reflection of what is actually happening? Yes they are stressed in that moment, but were they always stressed; what happened to make them experience stress? After all, stress is really just the misperception of strain. Two seemingly similar salespeople may, through the course of the job, be exposed to the same constant strain (carrying a sales target for example) but experience said strain very differently. For one salesperson it might be experienced as a challenge, accompanied with the satisfaction of pitting their ability against the measures of their role. Whereas for the other the large sales target is felt as a weight bearing down upon them to add further gravity to an already burdened situation. So what is that tipping point? When does strain becomes stress?

In translating what strain is we might describe it as a balance between the applied resources, acumen and ability possessed by the individual and the successful negotiation of the tasks and challenges being directed towards them. This situation, consciously or unconsciously experienced, is underpinned by the acknowledgement that the situation places the individual at the fulcrum of the two opposing forces.

This means that a salesperson managing strain acts with applied focus and energy, feeling it is possible to manage the workload and often finding enjoyment in attaining that balance. But that same person also recognises that without continued focus and awareness of what is being undertaken that balance could easily be lost and tip the weight away from equilibrium, thus changing from strain to stress.

The moment you feel you do not have sufficient resources, whether it be time, ability, opportunity or something else, you are potentially susceptible to the transformation of strain into stress. So when we view stress and strain in these terms it is not a question of "how one manages stress in the sales environment"; we can see this is simply just a change in perception of the event and functions of the job. If experiencing events is influenced by how we see things, and how we see things is affected or influenced by our state, it rather becomes a question of "how one can maintain a positive higher state" in order to better manage the strain rather than deal with stress.

Today it seems we cannot go more than a few clicks on social media without experts extolling the many benefits to be gained from exercise. Because of the extensive research that has been carried out we know much about the beneficial effects of exercise on the body. We know that other than conditioning the muscular and vascular systems aerobic exercise triggers change and beneficial mood-enhancing chemical production in our brains. To the brain that vigorous exercise is interpreted as a stressful event, which is likely a residual evolutionary reaction from our early ancestry, that fight or flight response you are probably aware of. As your heart rate increases, the brain thinks you are either fighting the enemy or fleeing from it. Anyone who has ever worked out knows if we push beyond the boundaries of our comfort zone we experience discomfort and pain. When that happens, in the brains of those who exercise regularly the body counters the pain by producing and releasing endorphins into their system, a chemical that counters the feeling of stress. In fact our endorphins' main purpose is to minimise the discomfort of the fight or flight, or in our case the exercise, blocking the feeling of pain. There are numerous cases, especially amongst runners, but accounts have been given by many other sportspeople, of a feeling, ranging from pleasant in some to euphoric in others, that can be experienced after running a certain distance.

The endorphins created within the brain to counteract the feelings of physical pain can effect a change in the mood and perception of the individual, with many reporting a feeling of invincibility and superior performance going beyond normal states of being, allowing them to produce extraordinary results when ordinarily the body would appear to have exceeded its ability. In an article he wrote, Yiannis Kouros, described by many as a legend in the world of ultra running, once explained what he experienced when he was running.

"Some may ask why I am running such long distances. There are reasons. During the ultras I come to a point where my body is almost dead. My mind has to take leadership. When it is very hard there is a war going on between the body and the mind. If my body wins, I will have to give up; if my mind wins, I will continue. At that time I feel that I stay outside of my body. It is as if I see my body in front of me; my mind commands and my body follows. This is a very special feeling, which I like very much. It is a very beautiful feeling and the only time I experience my personality separate from my body, as two different things."[7]

What Yiannis Kouros is saying is that when he is running for a long enough time his body and mind separate; he goes through a barrier to enter a peak experience or flow state and he is able to maintain with little to no discomfort the strain his body is enduring during the ultra marathons that he competes in.

Things don't stop there: the body being the wonderfully complex organism that it is protects you further from the effects of stress by your brain releasing other neurochemicals at the same time as endorphins. One particular protein called BDNF (Brain-Derived Neurotrophic Factor) is particularly useful in keeping the brain healthy. This particular protein has a protective and reparative function towards your memory neurons and acts as an internal automatic reset switch. The role played by BDNF is not just limited to state; research has revealed that it is crucial for memory function together with staving off neurological diseases including Alzheimer's and Parkinson's. We can see that regular exercise, apart from producing healthy bodies through the release of neurochemicals, can also influence the long-term health of the mind.

---

[7] Yiannis Kouros, 1990, "A War Going On Between My Body And My Mind", *Ultrarunning*, March 1990, p. 19.

So could we say the more exercise we do the better we function all round? Now here is where it gets interesting. An experiment conducted by researchers at Dartmouth College in Hanover, New Hampshire shed further light on the subject with interesting results. It was found that to be more productive and happier on a given work day, it didn't matter so much if you hadn't worked out on that particular day, as long as you worked out regularly:

"Those who had exercised during the preceding month but not on the day of testing generally did better on the memory test than those who had been sedentary, but did not perform nearly as well as those who had worked out that morning.

"The first 20 minutes of moving around, if someone has been really sedentary, provide most of the health benefits. You get prolonged life, reduced disease risk — all of those things come in in the first 20 minutes of being active."[8]

Science has revealed to us the principles of why exercising can make us happy, and what happens inside our brain cells during exercise. Further light is shed in research from the University of Bristol.[9] A research associate in the university's Department of Exercise, Nutrition and Health Sciences explains that they observed that on exercise days, people's mood significantly improved after exercising. Their mood or state stayed about the same on days they did not, with the exception of their sense of calm, which deteriorated. So we do not even have to exercise for long periods: as little as 20 minutes' regular aerobic exercise can afford us benefits consistent with a happier and healthier life.

---

[8] Dartmouth College, Hanover, New Hampshire experiment: Hopkins, M.E., Davis, F.C., VanTieghem, M.R., Whalen, P.J., and Bucci, D.J., 2012, Differential Effects of Acute and Regular Physical Exercise on Cognition and Affect, *Neuroscience* 2012, July, 26: p. 215. Available at: www.ncbi.nlm.nih.gov/pmc/articles/PMC3374855.

[9] University of Bristol study: J.C. Coulson, J. McKenna, M. Field, 2008, Exercising at work and self-reported work performance, *International Journal of Workplace Health Management*, 2008, 1(3). Available at: http://www.bristol.ac.uk/news/2008/6063.html.

The most important part to understand now is of course how you can reach this balance point, to attain your raised state in an optimal and longer lasting way. The intention here is to encourage you to incorporate into your daily practice an approach that enables you to access and remain in a higher energetic state for the day ahead. It is not about becoming a Zen monk, disconnected from the world around you. It's recognising that state-raising techniques like exercise can, when practised regularly, essentially condition your sense of wellbeing, and that conditioning equips you better to deal with the events and circumstances that invariably happen and might otherwise create internal stress, resentment and conflict, thus interfering with your ability to calmly and rationally deal with whatever happens. If you have any internal conflicts about what is happening around you some part of your awareness and corresponding available psychic mental energy is going to be diverted to manage or at least contain that conflict. So get some exercise, get moving around, energise your body and the mind will follow. Choose to make exercise a part of your state maintenance programme, but you will need to practise it for it to pay off.

Using exercise to elevate your state, bolstering your resilience to the events around you, is merely the tip of the energetic state iceberg. In recent years, and maybe as a reflection of the human condition constantly striving for improvement, there have emerged groups within society who have discovered the value and power of maintaining higher states for themselves. Unlikely as they are collectively, each in their own way, the scientist, the extreme sports enthusiast and the corporate executive of Silicon Valley have experienced higher energetic or what is being described as flow states in the pursuit of their passions. These flow states are being heralded as a portal to greater creativity, productivity and self-development in the work that we can immerse ourselves in.

A reflection of this today is found in the interest in and promotion of maintaining healthy mind states in the corporate world. Traditionally health of the employee has been more focused towards physical wellbeing, reflected in corporate gym memberships and wellness related healthcare plans offered as part of the employee's benefits package. Nevertheless, over the last 5 to 10 years the scope of the corporate employer in respect to wellbeing has widened, driven by further examination of how efficiency and productivity can be improved upon across every facet of the company environment. The cynical view could be that when the operational structure of the business cannot be tuned any further then attention logically shifts to the tuning of the employee's performance. The examination of state-changing practices to enhance employee performance in the corporate environment is really starting to be seriously explored and underpinned by genuine scientific interest.

Maybe it's simply because people represent a significant part of the corporate machine that the pursuit of new levels of enhanced performance, which has been surprising to some in the direction it is taking, is just a natural progression of those in industry that seek to disrupt existing paradigms in favour of progress. Alternatively, maybe it is just that western society today is more open and accepting of ideas of personal development historically associated with that of the spiritual seeker.

This is in part down to people like Martin Seligman, part of a new generation of positive psychologists. Their work in the world of optimum performance has taken the direction of repackaging meditation. By incorporating new state-changing tools and techniques into everyday lives, his approach and that of others like him is stripping back the esoteric and spiritual aspect to the practice in order to provide evidence-based validation for its benefits. Science, it seems, is now ready to explain the benefits of what many have taken on faith for centuries. Whatever route leads you to the practice of enhancing your state and wellbeing, surely it is the results that matter, especially if more productive flow states can be attained.

Science has already explored why exercise has therapeutic effects on the body and mind but other methods of reaching higher energetic or flow states are under the microscope. Now more than ever these new approaches for state change and the influences they can have on our performance are being adopted throughout the corporate world. Mindfulness-based stress reduction is being practised regularly by some 18 million people in the USA. If that isn't significant enough for you, what really reflects a paradigm shift in the corporate world is that by the end of 2017 over 40% of all US companies were set to be offering their employees mindfulness training because happy and healthy employees take fewer sick days and are generally more productive.

Flow and its importance

What is flow, and why is it essential? How much of your job do you really enjoy, what portion of it do you tolerate, and how much of it do you wish you didn't do at all? So much of what we call satisfaction from our role as salesperson, account administrator, financial forecaster, customer liaison officer and the multitude of other functions the modern day account manager undertakes is closely associated with how we can individually answer this question.

The reward which we receive, most commonly measured financially, is quite often the balancing component which not uncommonly counteracts an unnaturally disproportionate amount of dissatisfaction with what we do. Put bluntly, it is often seen as "the more money I make, the more I can ignore or overlook the aspects of the job I dislike". Now the problem here is that this coping strategy expends a large amount of mental energy as there is a continual conflict running which is exhibited in many cases as denial about how we really feel, and this in itself leads to other problems, and over time can easily lead to dysfunction in and outside of the job such as a drop in performance, loss of interest in the work or, quite possibly for some, an increase in consumption of alcohol or worse drugs.

Let us start by examining those aspects of the job you enjoy. Have you ever given any thought to what they are or why are they enjoyable to you? Are they the meetings, the presentations, or maybe the processing of orders? Which activities that you undertake as part of your role would you, on balance, rather be engaged in more of compared to other tasks in the workflow?

Looking back over my experience and examining the underlying aspects of why I enjoyed doing what I did, I noticed some consistent elements to the task at hand and the sense of enjoyment and satisfaction from it. Attending first meetings was always something I enjoyed. During those early engagement meetings, the ones where you might get a sense of great opportunity just beneath the surface of what's being discussed, I was able to connect strongly with clients, with rapport being established with little effort, and a fluid exchange of information and ideas taking place. On many occasions over the years I would be surprised how time during those meetings seemed to pass so quickly, as if the meeting happened in no time at all but in fact nearly two hours had gone by. Incidentally that never seemed to occur during unproductive meetings or the more laborious aspects of the job.

Is that sense of "time, no time" ever present in the work you engage with? Maybe it's far more noticeable the other way, when time seems to drag on with a minute that feels like an hour, normally when you want to be elsewhere or doing something different when you are not present and engaged with where you are.

Looking deeper into that experience, into the why behind the enjoyment, I recognised that the satisfaction from meeting prospective clients was really from an opportunity to add value to the situation. This might have been sharing of industry insights, working together to optimise network architectures or finding a common understanding that might lead to the development of a new business relationship, but all of them were aspects that I felt reflected some of my strongest skills, and maybe it was because I was able to use those skills of qualification, communication and rapport building that I was much more engaged.

I was very much motivated by that sense of potential just beneath the surface of the situation, the potentiality of opportunity waiting to be uncovered. I genuinely did believe and still do that every meeting has the potentiality of being the start of a great relationship, potentially leading to great deals being struck. I guess I never lost that sense of possibility. Now admittedly I was, and remain, a huge advocate for the practice of strong qualification within my teams. There was always a strong alignment of requisite details prior to attending any meeting with team members, reducing the potentiality of the meeting being a "poor use of my time", which further added to the sense of potential with every engagement. So the overall feeling of enjoyment with what I was doing, what I was focused on, absorbed in, could be described as being in flow.

The consequences of flow states are often described as producing our best work and our clearest thoughts, and it comes almost effortlessly. A flow state is something you experience; it's nothing that can be "found". The moment you start to look for it you have made it into an object and that becomes the focus of your energy and attention, drawing you away from the task, activity or situation. So if we cannot actively look for it, how do we recognise it?

We recognise it when doing something fun, be it work or play. It is far more likely that you encounter flow outside the office. It's far more easily entered into whilst having fun, doing stuff you enjoy which tends to be stuff you are good at or at least have a strong desire to become good at, like learning a new activity or playing sports. But there is a contradiction here: when you are truly enjoying yourself, are you really aware that you are having fun at the time? Does the idea of "I'm having fun" come from a point when you break with the experience? Pausing for a moment to take stock of what's happened, are you ever thinking you're having fun whilst in the moment or just experiencing it?

During a sales presentation if you feel in complete control of your performance you're not thinking how great you are doing in front of your clients. When you're playing a game of squash, returning the ball with precision, you're not reflecting that this is your best play. In those situations you are immersed in the moment, unaware of yourself. You are simply engaged with what you are doing, and that is why your best performance flows through. That said, in both scenarios, on occasions during both the meeting and the squash game, I have lost that connection with the moment, becoming aware of myself or rather self-conscious, missing the mark with the return serve on the squash court or losing the flow of the presentation, not necessarily to a disastrous end, but merely noticing the change in my inner state, the flow of my communication.

Sometimes we describe those incidents as nerves, stage fright or lapses in concentration. After all, concentration is directing your attention and energy towards a single point of focus, is it not? It's only after the meeting that you take stock of the quality of the exchange, the value of your impact in the room. Only outside of that focus do you form a value judgement about the event or experience; it's when you start thinking about it that you say to yourself "Hey, that was great, that was fun". That is not to say you aren't getting immediate feedback as to your performance in whatever you engage in but it is feedback that is sensed rather than framed by a value judgement.

Features of flow states

What are the characteristics of flow states? One way in which encountering flow states is marked is by having *clarity of purpose* and clear objectives, not limited to the end goal you are moving towards but clarity moment by moment. You know why you are where you are, and what is required from you; whether in the meeting or writing the proposal you are clear on what you are seeking to accomplish. You have clarity of purpose.

The second is that the awareness of your progress and the feedback you receive from what you are doing is *immediate*. Everything actioned is either moving you forward or it's not. You can sense or visibly see a progression and positive consequence in your endeavours. When writing a document the words flow, forming a cogent, salient proposition articulating the key strengths of your message with the value to the client being evident. Discussing solutions with clients where verbal and non-verbal feedback to what you are conveying is clear and serving as a real-time measure as to the efficacy of your words, you sense the resonance with what you are communicating. This sense of fluidity is always immediate.

A better way to describe the flow of immediate feedback might be the pianist playing a piece of music. During the recital a single wrong note is immediately recognisable because it doesn't keep the flow of the larger piece. The feedback to the musician is instantaneous. Ask yourself, can you recall an instance when you have experienced that degree of feedback in something you have done? This may not be in the work environment but may be when playing a sport or learning an instrument. For example, that total awareness of the air moving in and out of your lungs as you breathe into a saxophone, or the way your muscles contract and then flex when reaching out to return the ball during a game of tennis, and if that flow state is encountered, in those instances another characteristic associated with flow might be noticed.

Have you ever played a sport, practised an instrument, or maybe worked all night on a project, completely unaware of your own sense of fatigue? You were so engrossed in the activity you didn't realise you were tired until you broke your concentration, interrupting your focus, and you remembered that you had been working, playing, or practising for hours. It's that interruption that sparks the thought, that you should be tired or hungry, and then you realised the fatigue or hunger.

Most people have experienced this even if it was just once: that sense of *no time passing*, no hunger felt, no fatigue slowing the mind and body down. It's that momentary astonishment of losing four hours to an activity, the fact you have not eaten all day or that you have been awake 20 hours straight! That is a very good indicator that you have been in flow with whatever it is you have been doing. This is not necessarily something you will experience with ease or immediately, but these characteristics point to what is possible when you completely engage without resistance with whatever you are working on. I am offering them here as what is possible when practising the maintenance of high states of energy and focus.

As I asked you at the beginning of this book, please do not take my word on any of what is put before for you; I offer it here as a starting point for your own investigations. Question what is placed before you, do further research and reading, but question it in the context of your own experiences. Ask what your experiences might be true of in relation to what you have read: do they point towards what others have encountered? Be your own proof. The validation is so much more powerful when you encounter the proof experientially. I say this because it's human nature to want evidence when we are being presented with something that we are being invited to accept or believe in.

This is especially so when it comes to undertaking a practice that will require commitment of personal resources, be it monetary or time and energy. It is absolutely no accident that McDonald's has used the slogan "McDonald's – Billions Served" in its advertisements as it speaks to the doubt in each of us and reassures us that the choice has been encountered and made by a billion plus people before you and that it's a safe bet. It taps into the way we evaluate risk and make decisions. Continue with an open mind and seek your own experience.

Getting into flow at work

So how do we actually get into flow states during our working life, because playing sports or some other fun recreational activity is much simpler to get immersed in, isn't it? After all, it's play and not work. The key words here are play and fun. Maybe it's because we have an ingrained idea that work is, well, work, and unless you are amongst the lucky few that see work differently, to many work is something that must be done so as to function in society. We might have chosen our career path on the basis of what we were good at at school, expanding further in college or university, to then choose a stable or lucrative career. Maybe I am wrong but many choose their career on the basis of what will provide the most rather than what they might enjoy the most.

The irony perhaps then is people's work may be doing something they like or dislike to varying degrees and once their basic needs are met like food, rent and other functional living expenses they then use what they have left of their money and time to do the stuff they enjoy doing, unconsciously doing stuff that gets them into a raised state. Don't you feel good about things that really engage you, such as playing sports, listening to music or being lost in endless conversation in the pub with your friends?

So the idea here, the key to discovering greater experiences of flow in your work, is to have fun with what you are doing. Don't limit it to the sales environment. Take this opportunity to make a list of what is fun for you and include why. In fact it will be helpful to us later on, when you get to Part 4 of the book, if included in the list are those work things that you routinely dislike doing. If you don't already have a clear idea start by asking yourself simply what do you do for play and follow the line of questioning from there. Such as, why you enjoy it, asking yourself what aspects are enjoyable. Does that list of things, when you are having fun, that's to say engaged in the activity, make use of your strongest skills? There is a correlation between what we are good at and what we enjoy. Could it be true for you that the better you become at specific sales functions and activities the more enjoyment you can derive from them?

Reviewing the results of the exercise above, is there any correlation to this idea? That you enjoy most what you are best at, and that it makes use of your skills, whatever they are? Then ask yourself, are there any crossovers between what you enjoy doing when you play and what your top strengths are? When you can identify your top strengths you can start to explore how you might re-craft the way you work so that those capabilities, those things you enjoy doing, the elements that create the enjoyable experiences, can be integrated into your work situation.

Children's education is a good example: teachers incorporate learning into fun activities to hold their attention. Attention is held for longer when they are interested and engaged with the lessons. Of course it is easier to form patterns in the plastic-like minds of children, because they are not filled with all the subconscious programming of adulthood. All those ideas we have absorbed and integrated unknowingly, but it is not impossible to change our thoughts. If we can change our thoughts we can ultimately change anything as our thoughts become the structure for how we interact with the world around us.

This re-crafting of our sense of what work is starts to blur the boundaries that we have created in our mind about what it means to work and what we think about play. When we do this we start to merge the two distinct and separate mind-held concepts of work and play. A mentor has said to me on more than one occasion that he didn't feel as if he worked because when he did it felt more like play to him. He got so much more from the engagement with his business because he had recontextualised what it meant for him to work.

Have fun with your work! Set the intention to make a game of (have fun with) what you do day in, day out. As an exercise to discover more about this, take some time to examine where you might employ your best skills, writing down all the varying facets of your daily, weekly and monthly activities and then try to identify where your top skills (those aspects you enjoy the most about your work) are actually employed. Hold onto these results as you can use them for another exercise later on, in Chapter 10. Of those areas, tasks and activities, can you be clear in what way you use them during the activity? It might be that you can't find a way to incorporate key skills into all aspects of the job; data entry is a dry pursuit but our minds can be creative when tasked with a challenge and whilst it might be impossible to offer examples, your own attempts may yield far more enjoyable results.

Set yourself challenges, small at first, but set a challenge that moves you forward in your objectives or deepens the relationships with your clients or colleagues. Be clear on your skills and look at where you actually use them and then where you might further employ them in as many of your daily work activities as possible.

Try to be specific if possible. Maybe you love conducting new meetings because the meeting situation might allow you to generate rapport through disarming conversation, that in turn leads to an opening up of the opportunity. Does that same enjoyment dissipate at all for existing client meetings? If so, why is that? What is it about those first meetings you get enjoyment from? Is it the potential discovery of opportunity, the fun of crafting a great story and how it can add value to the client's business or something else? You need to examine your own experience to understand this. Alternatively ask yourself what is different about subsequent meetings or those tasks that you don't currently enjoy as much: what can you discern about those meetings or activities that changes the way you experience them?

If rapport building is a strength for you and something that gives you that sense of reward or achievement, something that can be experienced as fun when you excel whilst doing it, then look to see how that can be incorporated into the other meetings, activities and tasks.

With whatever you set out to accomplish, give yourself every opportunity to achieve it. If you have a number of calls planned with clients, challenge yourself to add a new dimension to the exchange. Of course you know your clients and so to a large extent the exchange normally takes place on the terms that were tacitly set when you first started interacting, but the best relationships reflect growth and development that takes place during the relationship and it comes with the desire to serve and provide great service. Be prepared to push yourself, to explore and expand the current boundaries of the relationship so as to improve upon it in whatever way you recognise that improvement as being. Maybe you feel the call with client X is not particularly relaxed or is perfunctory in nature; that is not necessarily a bad thing, but consider why your relationship with your client is the way it is.

What set those conditions on how you now interact? Use your strengths, those skills you enjoy using, to grow the relationship beyond where it is and enjoy the undertaking as much as the result. Maybe broaden the scope of what is normally discussed. If it's not a normal part of your dialogue then consider sharing new or impactful industry intelligence as a point of relevant discussion in the exchange. Or it might be adding more humour, discovering something of your client's interests or life outside work. Proposing a different venue for your meeting instead of the usual format may also help with the shift in the way you communicate.

Of course there is a balance to be struck and it is not always possible to interact with your clients other than in the way you currently do, but you do need to keep trying different approaches. Yes, you are on the call or in the meeting for a specific reason, but taking a genuine interest beyond the normal parameters reflects a deeper aspect to yourself and you may just discover that your client's behaviour to you is simply a mirror of your own. All it might take is the change in you and your approach to trigger the start of change in them.

Of course you may well be thinking this is all a given and not a new idea, and no it is not, but are you entirely happy with the interactions with all your clients and colleagues, or have you reached a plateau? Bring conscious awareness to the exchanges that take place within your accounts. Observe how your meetings unfold. Are they always the same; do your calls essentially run the same way each time? Are you happy with the results of those calls? In the examination of your past performances it's important that you undertake the review dispassionately so that, when you become aware of something that you wish to change, you do not label what you were doing before as bad or wrong. Just practise non-labelling acceptance of where you were in terms of your activity or performance which no longer reflects where you choose to be.

With your clients, set yourself a challenge to better the exchange, add more value, whatever it is you offer. But have fun with it, match your skills and abilities, set yourself a challenge to get a client talking more freely beyond the immediacy of the agenda, whilst also accepting it might not happen in one instant. Relationships take time to develop and just like examining your own performance, for those clients and accounts that have the greatest potential for change, those which are far from where you would like them to be, let go of the need to label them as something other than what you would like them to become lest they live up to that expectation. Put differently, if you label the account and client as closed, unfriendly, difficult or any other way of being contrary to your ideal then you are going to subconsciously look for evidence to support that judgement and you are less likely to break past that mindset. All I am suggesting is that on a daily basis you give yourself the greatest opportunity by playing your best hand and enjoying the game you're playing.

So given what we know, this puts us in an interesting situation. Now that we are aware of the differences in state and the potential benefits flow can have on our self and the way we are seen, why would you not consciously raise your state?

On any given day, be vigilant to any negative emotion or thought that may arise and which you hold onto whilst going about your day. Even if it is a minor irritation, like someone failing to acknowledge you for holding the door open for him or her as they walked through. Even if it is in the back of your mind (it need not be right in the forefront of your awareness), just having that background feeling affects your state; it takes energy to hold onto irritations and even more energy to remain angry, all of which can impact the quality of your work. Annoyances and frustrations will at some level carry a negative undercurrent, one that will filter your perception or experience of events that turn up, both small and significant.

So let us briefly go back to John, our deflated account manager. The simple answer to our question, of what John could have done differently, is to recognise that you invariably cannot change things after they have happened. You can, however, change the way you relate to them, by just letting go of whatever got under your skin by recognising no good can come from holding onto it. So doing allows you to deal with and move on from events far more effectively and calmly without the strain of daily life turning into a succession of minor stresses punctuating your day.

Chapter Summary

Life is a Canvas

- Break the stream of continuous unconscious thought by frequently asking "Am I present?" throughout the day.
- Maintain your highest state to better manage the strain of your daily workload thus avoiding its transformation into stress.
- Make state-raising and state-maintaining practices part of your daily routine.
- Be clear on what you enjoy doing at work and why.
- List your strongest skills and how they are used in the fulfilment of your duties.

Part 3 - Intention

We have looked at how raising your state and being in a state of flow can positively impact your life and work. Letting go of what no longer serves you is a big step towards the realisation of your desired outcomes, because you are no longer consuming vital energy maintaining or containing disruptive conflicting ideas about how things should be. This follows onto the second Point of Conscious Performance, intention. We will explore why it is important to set clear intentions for activities or tasks where you wish to experience a change from the previously observed outcomes.

Set intentions underpin conscious actions, actions which must be taken to advance you from where you are to where you want to be. This section will highlight what kind of underlying thought patterns are in play when you go about your day and what impact they can have on you mentally, physically and chemically, and how we can start to change habitual experiences and install positive, enabling belief structures.

Chapter 8 – The Human Memory

Setting off from a consciously maintained higher state, the sales professional is placed on the road to their desired success. The desired signed contract is still a long way from the starting point and like any journey a destination must be chosen. The sales process must successfully traverse a number of stages, each marking progress in the sale.

Setting plans is setting intentions

In "Service as a journey", back at the beginning of Chapter 3, I posed two questions: whether you and your client shared the same sales journey destination and secondly, how many of those tasks and activities associated with the sales process and the opportunities you are engaged in do you actually set a plan for in order to reach that desired destination of success? That setting of a plan is essentially setting an intention.

Let us start with a look at setting intentions for each task undertaken. To be clear there is a distinction between the setting of an intention and doing various activities associated with the sales cycle. Following your qualification steps, opportunity reviews and plans of actions are all a given necessity.

Ask yourself, what were your intentions when getting up and going to work today? Did you actually have any? Setting an intention is like drawing a map of where you wish to go — it becomes the driving force of your subconscious mind. Without an intention there is no map, and you're just travelling down a road without a destination in mind, or worse still you are reading from a very outdated map, one that repeatedly returns you to a past destination, a destination you don't actually want to visit.

For many salespeople basic tasks like attending meetings, designing solutions and writing proposals are all key components of their regular activity. Whether it's researching a new potential client company or meeting with an existing account contact, in the absence of a specific intention being set, automatic intentions or at least previous experiences from within the subconscious will have kicked in before you have even engaged. Those subconscious intentions or old patterns of behaviour will mostly likely have either influenced or determined your experience and outcome without you being aware of it. These behaviours may have been set way back in the past, maybe even years. Have you thought about which map you are reading from?

Many of the ideas we hold as sales professionals about our best or most efficient working practices are based upon our experiences along with the influences of our peers and leaders. Typically the deeper rooted ones emanate from our formative years when we were first starting out in the sales environment. At a time when habits and beliefs about the nature of effective selling are formed, or maybe not, it is possible the early experiences we had were not all entirely positive.

With the right environment and direction we are capable of cementing positive belief structures that will form the solid foundations of our sales practice and ultimately help carry us throughout our career, if we are fortunate, that is. If we are not, we continue down the road collecting various ideas and experiences stored as memories about the sales environment and ourselves, some of which do not serve us, with some of these ideas actually forming limiting beliefs.

Where did you get that idea that you were a strong closer, but creating account plans was not your best skill? Or that opening up dialogues and opportunities comes naturally in a 1 to 1 situation but you find it very challenging to stand up and present to larger groups of people? If you have any such thoughts can you see these are only ideas, ones you hold onto? They are not real. They may feel real because you made them by consistently energising them, that is to say reinforcing them by subconsciously remembering the emotion of the sponsoring event even if the details are not explicitly recalled.

This unconscious remembering combined with the way in which you consciously declare to yourself or others the limiting belief you happen to subscribe to is why it remains firmly in place as a limiting belief.

These limiting "ideas", left unaddressed or rather not "cleared" from the mind, easily become rigid "beliefs". Maybe the first time you stood up to present at a client meeting you dried up, choked on your words, forgot what to say or generally found the experience uncomfortable. The embarrassment or negative emotion that you then associated with it registered in your subconscious mind; over time it became fixed which is not surprising given that these can be powerfully charged experiences at a time when you are very receptive, seeking to absorb information.

Post the sponsoring event, the event that creates the association between activity and emotion, there then remains a subconscious link to that past event every time a similar situation arises. You may have continued to deliver presentations or carried on with cold calling for years ahead but your efficacy in these pursuits was potentially impaired to varying degrees because of the subconscious association to a strong negative emotion that to varying degrees got played out. As the emotion, which is the body's response to a thought, becomes lodged in the subconscious part of the mind the conscious mind accepts it as a limiting belief, unaware that it's self-created rather than realising what it actually is: just a negative feeling towards an old activity now being replayed to you by the subconscious mind.

What is very interesting is that the mind is actually attempting to enhance our performance in the situation by providing a frame of reference derived from our previous experiences. The mind is an amazing tool with an endless capacity to seek and recognise patterns, sourcing the closest resembling experiences (memories) and then, based on those previous experiences, preparing you mentally and physically for the activity.

The mind seeks to deliver a memory and relative emotion, which can be experienced as a feeling that will best equip you for the activity. This is a process likely related to the fight or flight response stimulated from within the older part of the brain we know as the limbic system. The limbic system supports a variety of functions including emotion, behaviour, motivation, long-term memory and olfaction, the processing and sensing of taste and smell. Emotional life is largely housed in the limbic system, and it has a great deal to do with the formation of memories.

To offer a more explanatory view of why the emotional echo of past experience is manifesting, not as an explicit memory with exact detail, rather an emotional reliving of the experience, let's look at the structure of memories. It is also worthy of note that to varying degrees the strength of memories may be dependent upon the individual and the intensity of the emotional charge at the time of the memory being formed.

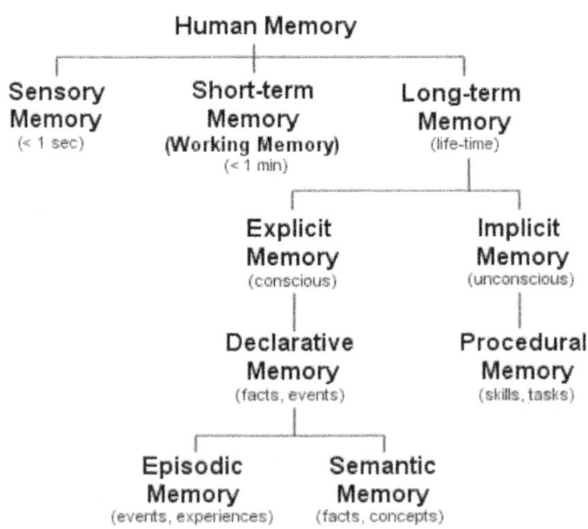

In the diagram above we can see the mapping of human memory structure. Note the implicit memory branch of the long-term memory. Implicit memory is also referred to as unconscious memory or automatic memory. Implicit memory draws upon past experiences to remember things without thinking about them. The performance of implicit memory is enabled by previous experiences, no matter how long ago those experiences occurred. This memory function of the brain and its subset is incredibly useful and allows us to navigate through daily life without expending huge mental effort to undertake the simplest of tasks. Everyday activities such as walking or getting dressed are made possible without having to give them thought due to a subset of implicit memory. The recall of these tasks is known as procedural memory, a memory function involved with the learning of new motor skills.

Without this aspect of memory function we would be unable to perform many everyday physical activities. The majority of implicit memories are procedural in nature but not all. This is why it's possible that you may experience feelings or emotions associated with a memory, that is, to be reliving the emotional experience of a past encounter every time you undertake an activity that triggers the memory without actually remembering the sponsoring event or, as is termed within the field of neuroscience, the encoding and storage of the event. To the experiencer, it seems that it is the current situation which is responsible for bringing forth the encountered emotions, feelings and ideas in response to the undertaking of an event, and not a deep subconscious link to a past event.

Through the lens of information and experience processing, the encoding refers to the way the brain interprets incoming stimuli and combines the processed information – the way we experience our reality – and the ensuing storage of the experience as a memory. Easterbrook's work describing cue utilisation theory has provided further insight.[10] Easterbrook's work predicted that high levels of arousal would lead to attention narrowing. Defined as a decrease in the range of cues from the stimulus and its environment to which the organism is sensitive, according to his hypothesis, attention will be focused primarily on the arousing details (cues) of the stimulus, so that information central to the source of the emotional arousal will be encoded whilst peripheral details will not.

---

[10] J.A. Easterbrook, 1959, The effect of emotion on cue utilization and the organization of behavior, *Psychology Review*, May, 66(3), pp. 318–325.

This can be interpreted as the strength of an emotional reaction to a specific aspect of an event or situation being experienced. This would lead to a reduction in the awareness of less meaningful or irrelevant aspects of what happened, resulting in storage of the dominant details of the experience as a memory and associated emotion. Accordingly, several studies have also demonstrated that the presentation of strong emotional stimuli (compared to neutral stimuli) results in enhanced memory of the core details (which can be seen as details central to the meaning of the emotional event) and impaired memory for peripheral details.

What research has further shown us is that strong emotional experiences such as embarrassment, humiliation or any of the difficult experiences one could conceivably encounter during the formative years, are far more likely to become a permanent record of the emotion and experience. Studies have shown that over time non-specific neutral memories decrease, that they fade away, whereas emotionally charged events remain the same or even improve, which could be an explanation as to why people's phobias such as public speaking seem to increase in intensity as time passes. It also points to why I have heard and said myself that the longer you leave getting back in the saddle of a task or activity you dislike or have avoided the harder it becomes to overcome the internal resistance.

How the mind stores and recalls memories and emotions points to a better understanding of how past experiences can interfere with interpretation of present moment reality. We can now start to clearly understand the forces at work and how it is possible that something that happened a long time ago, something we had all but forgotten about, was still exerting an influence on a daily basis together with how that influence is processed and rationalised by the conscious mind as a limiting belief. This is not the complete picture, however: there is another dimension to the experience and that is the physical one, and that is the effect on the body of reliving the emotion.

This chemical communication is the key premise of the later research of Candace Pert, an American neuroscientist and pharmacologist who discovered the opiate receptor, the cellular

binding site for endorphins in the brain. In her wor
of Emotion[11] she presents the idea that the hu
chemical signature to the emotions we experien
described in a simple experiment where it was demonstr
spoken words, when heard, trigger a thought, which can have
emotional and physical response. The test was carried out at a speaking engagement where the female facilitator called upon a young man from the audience to join her on the stage. The young man, a little uncertain as to what was going to happen, joined her on stage and was presented with a question. Addressing the whole room she asked him, "How many men does it take to put down the toilet seat?" A look of puzzlement appeared upon the young man's face; he replied he did not know, to which the facilitator said, "None, as it has never happened" and there followed a roar of laughter from amongst the audience, but rather more interesting was the automatic and uncontrolled response the young man had.

Pert explains that upon hearing the question, he processed it as a thought, and upon hearing the punchline that thought created an emotion, one of his embarrassment, which was then communicated throughout his body as an emotional and chemical response: the joke at his expense made him blush. What caused the man to blush was his response to a thought, which became an emotion that played out as a feeling with a physical manifestation. It's why some of us have gone red in the face when all eyes have been upon us during that presentation, that difficult meeting where we feel on the spot, or any other time when we become self-aware of our physical response to a situation.

As I have said before, our ideas and experiences, those with strong negative associations, get stored as emotional links within the subconscious mind; there they stay dormant until a situation arises where the mind calls upon the memory at a later date. It is possible these negative emotional experiences are processed and expressed as "I can't" or "I don't like" beliefs, thus further strengthening their anchor in our mind.

---

[11] C. Pert, 2000, *The Molecules of Emotion*, Simon & Schuster UK, pp. 846–848.

ıost of the time we are not even aware of the link. Humans have a great capacity to bury things deeply when we do not wish to consciously relive or address them. Therefore, unless you clear these ideas and associated emotions as they arise or replace them with stronger intentions, intentions that you reinforce regularly, a practice that will ultimately uproot the old belief, you will continue to repeat to some degree the experience of the past every time you find yourself in a similar situation.

That said, an old emotion cannot be forced out nor a new intention in and we will cover the clearing of old thoughts and emotions later in the chapter. Any intention you set is a seed that you have to sow and then let germinate and grow independently. You water it by consciously energising the belief that it is achievable, together with ensuring that kinaesthetically you are congruent with the new intention. Any body language or postures from an old paradigm should be observed, identified, and replaced.

What does that mean? Start by looking at your body language, what your body is doing in any situation you seek to improve upon. Once I arranged for a company to come in and work with our senior management team and leading salespeople. They were brought in to help us all become better communicators when presenting to audiences of differing sizes. A lot of the larger bids we were taking part in required members of the senior management team to participate in board presentations. Now it is a common mistakenly held belief that just because someone is in a senior leadership role they are going to be a naturally strong speaker. As the participation of the management team was becoming more commonplace in our corporate closing presentations we needed an improvement in the efficacy of the messages we delivered.

We all achieved this in varying degrees by being acutely aware of the way we stood, the pitch and pace of our speech and the way we each emphasised the message being delivered. In order for us to become aware of ourselves, part of the programme involved video recording our presentations. It is worth also adding that underpinning any successful presentation there must be the strength of your material and your belief in it. I strongly assert the importance of your intellectual property, the knowledge you possess which has formed the material you deliver: without this your foundations are on shaky ground. So taking confidence in the subject matter and presentation material as a given, what was most surprising to many during this training was the way in which the body seems to behave independently.

For example, at that time, whilst I wanted to improve my skills I held a belief that I was already a good presenter. It was therefore quite surprising to observe unconscious body behaviours such as touching my head, or an unconscious arm movement that did little to enhance the presentation during its delivery. This was surprising because, like my colleagues, we were unaware of it as it was happening until we became more aware of ourselves through reviewing the material on video.

Now it is not likely that it will be practicable to video the activities you engage in, however just bringing the dimension of awareness to them, the idea that you are observant of your actions, will immediately have an impact. Just be aware of what you are saying and doing, but do not judge any of it; just observe. Start by choosing one activity, one task to start with, and so as not to become overwhelmed, I also suggest it should be non-client facing. Ask yourself before the activity you wish to see changes in, "Do I have a routine? Do I stand in the same way every time, am I unanimated, do I always sit down in the same posture?" Try to identify what your normal operating pattern is when you start the task.

It's likely that when you look at the way you start the activity, for an example let's pick an easy one, making phone calls, you start them in the same manner every time. Maybe you have a routine, or is it even ritualistic? Don't laugh; some people cannot start anything until they have had their coffee, adjusted their seat, cleared their desk or other such activity. It's whatever is a "normal pattern" that you, the individual, feel has to take place for you to be in a mental position to undertake certain tasks. For those of you that are generally comfortable with how you operate, if you are bringing greater awareness to what you are doing and how you are carrying tasks out, you may become aware of behaviours previously unobserved, ones you may wish to change to allow greater effectiveness.

Breaking paradigms

So if you do not like being on the phone whilst sat at your desk, then set the new positive outcome intention followed by a change in your physicality: try standing up at your desk when dialling. I do believe this works.

As an example of changing physicality to assist in the supplanting of limiting beliefs, I remember the time when I ran the graduate sales team at a previous company. A principal part of the graduate role was to make calls into prospect and existing accounts and identify opportunities. It was evident that many graduates were very self-conscious when it came to being on the phone. By self-conscious I mean there appeared to be a lot of fear or anxiety about being seen or heard to be saying something wrong, or getting flustered, or forgetting what to say etc. These were all bright people and they would adopt a similar approach to making phone calls. I observed this many times; it started with the call being made at their desk with their body leaning forward almost hunched over the desk, most likely in an attempt to make themselves smaller, so as not to stand out, not to be seen or heard by the other salespeople on the floor.

Accompanying this posture would be a voice that may have started strong and with purpose, typically because they were reciting a well-rehearsed script, but on occasion their voice would start to decrease in volume and a correlating reduction in energy was noticed. This was often in response to calling an unreceptive person or if they had inadvertently gone off script and were uncomfortable with their level of knowledge on the topic being discussed together with the questions they were trying to field.

As part of their mentoring they were encouraged to recite their calling scripts to a level of perfection so that they owned the words, and felt utterly comfortable in what they were saying, but it did not always work. They would practise continually, become fluent, able to deliver the carefully crafted value proposition to other members of the team perfectly, and then after a short period of time the calling style started to revert to the old behaviour which was recognised as something that would make or break them as a sales professional.

At that time the mechanics of what was happening was not that clear; rather it was intuition that led me to take steps, knowing that if they could not lose their self-consciousness and just get on with the calling no amount of practice or studying was going to help because they were caught in a feedback loop. So I undertook an approach, one not to everyone's approval or liking, as a way of breaking the behavioural paradigm. I decided to take away their chairs. This may seem harsh, but by forcing them to stand up they had to face the realisation that they were going to be visible. They were going to be seen and heard and quite likely seen and heard getting it wrong. What they needed to learn was that it was ok to "get it wrong", and it was this that they really needed to understand.

To the graduates it was an uncomfortable, almost painful, experience, but they all realised quickly that the discomfort, the pain they encountered soon melted away as they got into what they were focused on, which was making calls, and not thinking about how they were being seen by others. The truth is, and you may all have a good idea as to what I mean, the feeling of discomfort never killed anyone; it just bruises the ego, which pretty soon recovers, albeit a little bit smaller for the experience. Once the grads had overcome their fear I gave them their chairs back. The irony of course is the ego within can swing like a pendulum, from one extreme of hiding away at the desk to the other extreme of a confident standing pose ensuring people can see and hear them.

In making them stand up whilst calling, what was actually happening? Apart from making them acutely self-aware.

Well, to start with the pain aspect of the experience, the discomfort, actually serves an important purpose, an idea which we will explore a little further on in Chapter 9. Why did standing up help these guys overcome their roadblock? Well you cannot breathe easily whilst hunched over. By standing up you open up your diaphragm, breathing more deeply, thus giving yourself plenty of oxygen, which aids in relaxation and allowing you to speak fluidly and with greater clarity. More importantly, though, is the fact that you are changing the engagement pattern for the activity, reducing the immediacy of recalling the old behavioural cycle or emotional memory. The mind does not immediately recognise the activity and therefore leaves space for a new experience to take place, one that is not experienced through the filter of the previous undertakings. Instead the space created allows for a new set intention to have a bearing on the experience as it unfolds. You have an idea of where you want the situation to go and because there is a map to follow it becomes less likely that you will move towards the past outcome.

Changing your physicality, your posture, in context to the task of changing paradigms is the lesser of the changes available to make. The principal driver of a new experience is setting a supplanting intention.

Making your intentions clear

When setting intentions, be clear on what you would like to achieve in your day. Define specifics, visualising the desired outcomes. Today as part of my work practice I spend a few minutes at the beginning of the day visualising the events and tasks of the day, as I would have them unfold. The more detail you can envisage the better, as you have a more accurate target of your energy and focus. I also suggest you start the process from the higher *state* previously explored and hopefully reached through your adoption of the techniques described in Chapter 6. There is also another important dimension to the practice of setting any intention. As we set an intention we are offering our subconscious mind a peek at a potential reality we wish to encounter. We set the intention by creating a colourfully rich image or mind movie of whatever it is we wish to bring about. The extra dimension of creativity to this is to imagine the feeling of the successful outcome as well.

How would you actually feel if what you envisaged for yourself came to fruition? If what you wanted for yourself came about you would undoubtedly experience some emotions, right? Lock the feeling of a successful outcome to your intention in order to more securely anchor the intention in the subconscious mind. This is actually really important as we very rarely encounter events we have hoped, wished or planned for devoid of any emotion, so it makes sense, if we are creating an intention, that the intended outcome of our actions must include the emotional element to it. You might have some resistance to this, and you might feel silly doing this, but this is a dimension of creating strong intentions. Practise feeling the success when picturing your desired outcome. The bigger the intention, the likelier you are to experience stronger positive emotions.

Set each intention individually

Set your intentions as to what the day will deliver. This need not be a laborious activity. Depending on how much time you have available you might try incorporating it into your waking practice by setting your alarm a few minutes earlier and investing that time to imagine the intention as it is unfolding in the movie theatre of your mind. Alternatively you could do the intention setting exercise the night before to benefit from it being the last thing you focus your concentration upon before sleeping, in essence ensuring that the intention is floating around in your mind for the entirety of your sleep. Wherever and however you choose to set intentions it is the detail you picture, the clarity with which the image appears anchored to the feelings of your successful outcome in your mind that's important.

Then, when you are ready to undertake the first task, take a few moments at your desk prior to commencing to clear your thoughts of all other matters, focusing on the one thing at hand in that precise and present moment. For those that find it difficult to still the mind, try taking several slow conscious breaths to help clear the mind space. This means focusing solely on the air entering and leaving the lungs; being mindful of this one thing will quiet your mind from any other thoughts. Don't believe it? Try it for yourself. Whilst engaged with the movements of your breath, try to think of something else at the same time. You cannot, because you will stop being focused on the breathing. If your entire focus is on your breath you will quiet your mind, and in that space you allow yourself stillness ready to set clear intentions.

Then set the intention desired again, just the intention for the activity you are to commence. Envisaging each and every component of the activity or task, how a conversation might transpire, what milestones may be reached and when. Visualise whatever it is you are going to engage in. So if you have the desire to complete three tasks in the day each should be prepared for in the same manner: each should be approached with a mind clearing, and visualisation.

Visualise the components of the exercise unfolding, holding in mind the relaxed yet creative delivery, the receptive nature of the person you are speaking with and the positive details you wish to discover and deliver. Once you have energised the intention and visualised the conversations do not revisit the intention; it has been set so simply let it go.

Your intention is a statement underpinned by your belief in a particular outcome, and it is much more effective when it comes from a place of belief in oneself and contentment that all is potentially possible, rather than set by an individual with an underlying feeling of lack, need, or who doubts the possibility of the outcome. It is also true that people who set powerful intentions remain in a positive focused state throughout. They stay centred and refuse to be influenced or affected by other people's doubts or criticisms.

The intention is the destination

Finally, relinquish any attachment to a specific result being brought about in a particular way, operating within the realm of uncertainty or, as I prefer to put it, from within the realm of super potentiality. I say this because it's the memory function/pattern recognition part of the brain at work again that is programmed to lead you astray. If you have set an intention and in the setting of that desired outcome you have visualised the way in which the outcome might unfold, you can easily fall into the unconscious trap of measuring everything you encounter against the visualisation you set, which can cause you to doubt the possibility of the outcome and create an internal conflict as to what is happening and what you should be doing.

The intention is the destination of a journey, and the visualising of the details serves to instil the belief that the outcome is possible; that's all. It's not the only way in which the outcome may manifest. But the mind will, if left unchecked, continue to measure and compare the current experience and the memory of the intention, which is why it is important to stay present and let go of the intention once it's set along with the idea that it must and can only come about in the way in which we envisioned it.

You have probably realised by now that for the most part the egoic mind, that is to say the voice in the head which places the sense of me, my, mine and I at the root of every sentence, is a constant. Rarely does the voice stay quiet for long. Maybe at times of intense focus it is still as your awareness and attention command all available mental energy, but mostly it's there waiting to start speaking to you or speaking at you, which is probably closer to the truth for the majority. The voice is ready to offer you both sides of a conversation, a conversation you are having with yourself. The voice can be helpful and other times it's a downright nuisance. But it is crazy, right? Surely I am not alone in thinking that? You too probably know that conversation in your head, the one where you are having both sides of the same conversation. It just doesn't make sense; it's happening in YOUR mind so surely you know what you are going to say. What really escapes me is why we then even have the conversation if we know what we are going to say! It's compulsive and draining.

But there can be respite; you can take back the control of your mind, because your mind – the voice in your head – isn't really who you are. Commonly we believe we are the voice but if you take a moment to consider that on those rare occasions when the mind is genuinely silent, in those moments when faced with something so far from the normal range of experiences, such as seeing a baby delivered into the world or witnessing a tragic accident, the egoic voice, the one that always places you at the centre of the universe, is silent.

In that silence you are what some describe as simply a field of awareness. It is then you realise that your mind, the egoic voice that almost constantly chatters, requires your conscious awareness for it to exist, but your conscious awareness does not require the mind's chatter to simply hear, see, touch and smell your surroundings. These are your core senses and do not require the mental running commentary in order for you to process and experience them. Commonly what takes place when we experience this thing called life is the continual overlay of the mind's commentary describing the world as the mind sees it and through the mental filters of your experiences rather than how it truly is. It's banal and often distracts the mind's focus away from the task at hand, if there is one, or otherwise just indulges in random thoughts. That constant narrative is the judgemental labelling we have explored previously.

The mental noise can and does surface again from time to time, offering its unwanted commentary on things casually observed or related to your activity. I am happy to say that for me the occurrence is far less frequent primarily due to the frequent practice of present moment awareness of my thoughts throughout the day. By this I mean simply bringing my awareness back to what I am thinking about, observing if the stream of thoughts and ideas are purposeful, or noticing when I have been lost in thought about some unimportant matter. The moment you focus your awareness on seeing that the current thought you are having is just noise, not relevant or attendant to what you are seeking to accomplish, at that moment you realise you are not being present. With that realisation you become present, and you will notice the noise just stopping. Having stopped your thinking and left a gap in the continuous stream of thought, you leave space for your unfiltered awareness to grow.

There have been times too numerous to recall when my mind ran away with itself, when it just had a constant dialogue running. In the past I was never comfortable in admitting it; maybe in some way I was fearful I was different to everyone else in the corporate world who seemed so well put together, that if people knew that I had this degree of mental noise in my head then I would be judged. So it was actually a relief when I realised I wasn't alone, and that to varying degrees nearly all of humanity is almost entirely identified with the voice in our heads. I say this with the hope that it connects with you and reiterate that you are not your thoughts or emotions; you are simply the witness to those thoughts and the experiences of the emotions related to the thoughts. Once this is truly understood you can actually free yourself from the repetitive thoughts that trigger the emotions that are the foundations of so many limiting beliefs.

Letting go of attachment

In the past I have planned journeys and something happened to force a change in the way that it was to be undertaken. Looking back it actually happened quite a lot when driving to meetings.

When we are not entirely sure of the route to take and if you are like me, someone without a natural sense of direction, we might use the map within our phone to guide us. It's also quite probable there will be more than a single route available to reach the destination.

We use phone apps because they make the journey simple; after all someone has done all the work, loading the app with all the roads, traffic lights, junctions, speed limits etc. They are all there, stored in the memory. All we need do is switch it on, enter the address of where we wish to go, and in no time we are offered the best route to the destination based upon where we are starting from. It's there on the screen with a voice speaking out the turn-by-turn instructions. But how many times have I tapped in the address and started off, only to question the route being offered by the app? On some occasions it seemed to me that the instructions being given were taking me in the wrong direction. Has that ever happened to you?

When that happens we are faced with a choice: continue driving as directed (trusting the device) or go in the direction we think is right because in our mind we have an idea of how it should be. In my head were just two points of view arguing for prime central position on which was right. I was saying to myself, "That's the wrong direction." My mind would then look to validate this particular view by remember something read somewhere online about people being given the wrong directions using satnav devices. I might even offer out loud something dismissive about the device. It's funny: even though I had accepted that I did not know the route to where I was going, and despite the satnav being designed to get me there, I still felt that I needed to start the journey off as if I was going in the right direction, the direction my mind thought I should be going in.

Of course what typically happened for me was that I would find the route offered went in a direction that was to avoid traffic, an accident or any other detail that would have incurred delays or problems to the journey. I know this because the route I thought better to take invariably got me stuck in traffic or other such delays.

So although it looked as if the route it was taking me was wrong, it was ultimately directing me to where I wanted to get in the most efficient way. It was just that from my perspective I had an idea of how the journey should unfold; I had an attachment to a particular route such that when it came to actually starting off I ignored the proffered path, because it didn't look like the right way, the way my mind pictured it to be.

How many times has that scenario happened to you in your experience? I don't just mean in the car. Investigate your own experiences, those instances when you achieved something, anything where you had an idea as to how it might unfold and then observed that it came about in a way you couldn't have foreseen. Or maybe you just resisted the situation because it did not meet your expectations as to how it should look or feel. It didn't match the way your mind's eye pictured it happening, so forcing you to question whether you were on the right path to your destination. Maybe you even abandoned whatever you were attempting simply because things were not moving in the way you expected.

Try not to get attached to how you think things should play out. Today I attempt to let go of that kind of attachment when I become aware of it. That's simply because in the myriad dimensions to any event of coincidence, those events that bring about an outcome which we define with a value judgement according to our expectation are so vast it is almost too big to hold in our mind. It is the seemingly random correlation of infinite moving parts that forms the fabric of the reality we experience: the picking up of a telephone or not, the catching the green light in the car or not, the conversation had in the meeting or not. All of these and everything else coalesces to create the experience, so if we can agree that there are infinite possible variations, that life is just a rendering of super potentiality, doesn't it seem rather peculiar that we should expect things, and be really attached to those things playing out in a particular way?

It's probably because we almost never consider it. A great example of the ripple effect in potential outcomes as a consequence of something as simple as missing a tube train is the 90s movie *Sliding Doors*, where the main character's life is depicted in the consequences and divergent paths it takes when she misses a tube train. The movie shows in true Hollywood style that the happy ending to the movie was always the outcome but the two versions of the journey the story offered were quite different.

Maybe we all take it for granted or never consider it, but think about it now for a few moments. Consider how many moving parts are in play at any given time just to bring two people together at a set time for a meeting. You start off on a journey to attend a meeting. To get there you normally take the underground but on this particular morning the tube is closed. You head above ground and jump on a bus; it takes you most of the way and then you finish the journey on foot, or maybe it was just one line of the underground which was closed, so you took a five-stop detour. You still got to where you wanted to get to but on that day the route wasn't the one you normally take. Did it mean that you questioned where you were heading, stopped and doubted that you were going to get there? Of course not; you checked the map, plotted an alternate route and off you went on your merry way.

So what's the difference between that analogy and your work life? Looking beyond the fact that you don't have a map on a wall to reference, what this scenario suggests is that from time to time our usual journey (and by that I mean anything where we have an expectation of the outcome being in a certain way), the one we have in our minds, is disrupted. For a lot of people this disruption to the expected outcome can be a source of frustration and even anxiety, especially when we place such value on the outcome.

Nonetheless it is entirely your decision to make the adjustment in your actions and thinking and get on with the journey. On a change of journey into work, would you continually judge the reroute as you undertook it, criticising yourself or what you were doing? Of course not; you have a degree of faith that the reroute will deliver you to your desired destination. So why then get attached to ideas about how business is going to get done; why do deals need to happen in a certain way?

Just let go of the idea of how you think it should happen and focus on each step you are taking. As soon as you take a step and if you stay vigilant, that is stay present, then the following step will become apparent for you to take, even if you haven't travelled that path before. You do it with the familiar things like travelling on the underground; the only difference is the attachment we have to the idea of how it will, should or must happen. You don't hold that attachment to a change on your journey to work because ultimately it's just not that significant. If we can let go of the attachment to or expectations of how things should be, we can move on with more of our energy directed to meaningful activity.

Through my own introspection I have come to realise that the root of my attachments for outcomes was based on fear and insecurity, whilst detachment is based on the belief in the power of the subconscious mind. I now intend for everything to work out as it should, then let go and allow opportunities and openings to come. I challenge you to try the same: explore why you are attached to the idea of your expectations. If you keep asking yourself "Why do I feel that?" you will ultimately arrive at your own truth about it.

Chapter Summary

The Human Memory

- Examine your ideas and beliefs about your weaknesses. Where do those ideas originate?
- Always set clear and precise intentions for each desired outcome.
- With every intention, attempt to experience the emotion of that intention coming to pass.

Chapter 9 – Passing through the Pain Barrier

Have you ever wondered why we suffer pain and discomfort? I have certainly asked myself that question on many occasions in the workplace. I have questioned why things were happening whilst at the same time trying to contain the numerous consequential emotions erupting from within, often a fluctuation between frustration and anger. It will be clear to you all that our working lives can potentially be a veritable cornucopia of pain. When I say pain I am not talking of the stubbing your toe type pain, or bouncing around the squash court with your manager trying not to keel over pain, no, what I am referring to which everyone experiences at some stage, to varying degrees, is emotional pain. The kind of thwarted wanting of a promotion, the pain of missing out on a deal, the embarrassment of a Monday morning sales meeting when you have a weak pipeline, the frustration that you have been treated badly by a customer, colleague or company; you get the picture.

Ok, so to a large extent I believe (and I feel there is plenty of evidence contained within here to substantiate this belief) that in this life the pain I speak of is entirely self-created. However I now see that what I previously felt as pain was simply a reaction to an external event that I processed through the filter of my state and level of awareness. This processing fed back to me an emotional interpretation of the physical and physiological levels of what was in front of me or what I might have been experiencing at that time. Ask any Buddhist; they will pretty much tell you the same.

So why do we do it? Why have we evolved to create this pain for ourselves, to interpret the events of our experience as in some way happening to us as if we were the subject of the situation rather than a witness to the event, even if we are subjectively involved? Is this really the correct functioning of the mind and body; is there really any point or purpose to it or have we all just evolved into a mentally and emotionally malfunctioning species? After all, wouldn't it be lovely if we could all enjoy an entirely pain-free work life, or an entirely pain-free life full stop, one that is always easy and never challenging? Well I think the truth of it is actually no, it would not.

If you disagree just take a moment. Ask yourself, is it a knee jerk "yes"? Would the reality live up to the idea? Just think about it for a moment and in the context of your work life, a role in which nothing challenges you, if there is no challenge how long could you maintain the level of service your clients command and the work ethic your employer expects? How long is it before you become thoroughly bored and neglectful of the care your job requires? The truth is, if we are not engaged by what we do we cannot engage with it, and any engagement must offer positive feedback from our input. This is broadly evident to all if we consider how we play games. As children we started off being happy to throw and catch a ball, but quickly we grew tired of such a limited interaction and reward. Through the development of our co-ordination and physicality we sought to make the game more complex, to attain more satisfaction from our time invested in play. This is something we explored in the section "Flow and its importance", back in Chapter 7. For now let's look at the experience of pain as a learning tool.

The pain you experienced didn't start out as pain, did it? Somewhere during the unfolding moments of your working day something started a change of your perception. Was it a word, an action or was it just an external event, one that precipitated a thought forming in your mind around the witnessed event? That thought was then expressed upon your body as an emotion that gave rise to a change in how you felt about whatever it was in front of you.

We know that stress (pain) is just our workload (strain) that has become out of balance with our available resources and the task in hand. We also know that we get our sense of achievement, our sense of job satisfaction, from the completion of tasks that have challenged us, so a life without challenge would be devoid of the psychological reward that most if not all of us look for. But that isn't how we interpret stress, because it's stress. It's stopped being strain and become stress and that's painful and we are conditioned to avoid experiences that are painful. I can remember times in my early career when I experienced strain turning into stress, mentally processed through my mind's filters, and suddenly the job I loved doing yesterday was an absolute nightmare today and "god only knows why I do it" and "maybe it's time to get out". Sound familiar? Ever said it, felt it or heard someone say it?

Ok so maybe, just maybe, if there were a purpose, a reason as to why we encounter pain, might that make it easier to deal with? Maybe it would help each of us to disassociate with the random ideas and thoughts created in our head around the events taking place, ideas and thoughts that take form which in turn can offer the mind some meaning for the emotions and "pain" experienced at any given time. This is important so we are going to break this one down. Before we explore the nature of pain and how it works let's examine the idea I just offered about how you potentially create the thoughts to explain the emotional state you may experience from time to time.

I can hear some of you saying, "Wait a minute, are you saying that we actually create things, ideas and situations to justify our emotions, to make sense of them? Uh uh, that sounds like crap."

Well that is how it sounded to me when I first heard it put that way. I have since changed my mind on it, and here is why. Remember back in Chapter 3 when we looked at how labelling events locked them into being whatever you perceived them to be at the expense of other potential outcomes? Well, why did you see the negative situation rather than any other outcome; why did you label it at all? And as I suggested before, your state, your inner energy level, directly affects your ability to perceive the events as they are, so the lower the state the lower the range of potential possible outcomes that may be perceived and manifest, and the higher the state the less likely you are to notice the little things, and the wider the range of potentiality from it.

If you are continually dwelling in the lower levels of your energetic state range then you are likely to be or have been affected by or experiencing something "negative", something sticky or heavy that as an emotion clings and is hard to shift, something not always at the forefront of your awareness. You know how we like to bury stuff, right?

Then when something else comes along, a triggering event, whatever it might be, that underlying feeling of negativity, the one in the background of your awareness, is able to bubble up and in order to make sense of this happening the mind slaps a great big label on the external event, one that matches the energetic signature of the negative emotion, then gives you a thought (value judgement) about the event that matches nicely to the negative emotion that has surfaced. Of course you don't see this or rather sense it as something that is happening; to you it is just one seamless experience.

Let's say the sales bid you have been working on was submitted but didn't get to the vendor on time and your company is excluded from participating in a big tender; ordinarily this is not a desired outcome but the way in which you respond to it and the emotions you experience which may include anger, blame, despair, self-pity etc. may be exaggerated. You may want to share your feelings about the unfairness of the situation, vent your spleen, tell your sad story to anyone who is there to listen. Those that do listen will be complicit in confirming the reality of your story. You may hear from them that some, any or all of your feelings are understandable given whatever circumstances have brought about the event, further justifying your interpretation of the emotion and event. So any lingering negative emotion of a similar essence, stuff you may be carrying from your past, is triggered by the external event and now bubbles up which is maybe why the emotion experienced is carrying a large charge and possibly evokes a disproportionate response to the event that appears to have caused it.

It is at this juncture that I believe we have fallen from the path. Our misjudgement and labelling only seem to compound the emotion surfacing rather than actually letting the emotion go, which is the purpose of the process.

This might be a difficult one for people to just accept, and actually I don't want you to. I would prefer for you to investigate within to find your truth of it. Ok, let's look at it this way. You are not your thoughts or your emotions. You have thoughts, you witness them, your body experiences the emotions, but they are not you; can we all agree on that? If like me you are asking, "But are we not just a sum of our experiences?" then the answer is both yes and no. We experience things all the time and to a large degree they frame how we perceive the world at large but this isn't necessarily a good thing all the time. Maybe we have got into the involuntary habit of holding on to some emotions and ideas picked up along the way. Thoughts and feelings that we hold on to which don't serve us.

Think about all the experiences you had today on your way into the office: the people you passed, adverts you saw, cars you heard, the million bits of data per second flying through your awareness. How many of those things did you experience and then decide to hold on to – a few, a lot? I can guarantee that it's a tiny number, whatever number you come up with, in respect to the total volume of data you experienced. Can you remember the number plate of the bus you caught or the hair colour of the train conductor? No, but you saw the bus approaching the stop and the ticket conductor checked your ticket. Your awareness would have seen the number plate or the conductor's face; it's just that you didn't choose to hold onto that detail, nor the million other details you encounter that pass right through you every moment to moment. There is no need to retain them, right; otherwise it would just start filling up your head with pointless details. These are just the inert things. They are the tiny details that make up the picture; they have no emotional charge to them, but what about the stuff we do hold onto, the stuff with charge; why does that linger?

To keep things simple let's use an analogy. In your head imagine there are two big boxes, called thoughts and emotions. When we have an experience that forms a thought we can, depending on the amount of focus we give to the thought, either throw it out into the garbage (let it go) or store it in the thought box (store it as a memory). As we know emotions are the body's experience of a thought manifested, so all those emotions go in the big emotions box, good ones, bad ones, happy, sad, excited, miserable etc. Now if like me you've been on the planet for over 40 years, let me tell you those boxes can get pretty full. So we have to get rid of the contents of the boxes; it is just not practicable or healthy to carry around all the negative thoughts and emotions we have picked up on our journey. So the subconscious mind, that wonderful complex aspect of ourselves, starts to say "we have got to get some of this junk out", and to achieve this all the conscious part of the mind has to do is remain open when the subconscious mind offers up a piece of emotional baggage for ejection.

Releasing the baggage

The conscious mind just needs to stay open and let it float off. That is to say, just let the emotion be there, to dissolve away, no labelling, no judgement. But, and this is the kicker, the conscious mind doesn't realise that the subconscious is bringing this stuff up so that it can be released. The purpose of bringing it up is to let go of it, but the conscious mind is experiencing this emotion and saying "What is going on? Ah, that event which just happened, I can use that to frame the experience of this emotion which I am now feeling, that fits, that makes sense and then I can chuck it back into the box after I have processed it (stewed on it for any period of time)." Of course this is suboptimal; the subconscious mind is trying to clear out stuff and make you lighter and the conscious mind is finding all manner of justifications to the experience and then chucking it back.

It's actually quite exhausting when you think about how long this situation has been going on. Then, from time to time, your conscious mind gets overridden and you have that brief moment of calmness witnessing an event that might otherwise have provoked anger from you, frustrated you or any other automatic response. In that calm moment, in that split second of stillness, you might say "You know what, I am just going to let that go" and in that moment you allow the emotion, which the subconscious offered up for clearing, you let it be there and it dissolves away.

Again I ask you to be the judge of this yourself. Think back in your experience: have you encountered a similar situation where you have just let go, stopped resisting what is and actually chosen for it to no longer have an energetic hold over your emotional state? It may have been a reaction to being cut up in traffic, a difference of mind with a colleague, or any other such situation when you had a burst of emotion and in a split second decided that it simply wasn't worth holding on to. You made a conscious decision that holding on to the emotion, feeling or mental position was not good for you and that it was just far simpler to let it go without creating more drama for yourself. For me when that "letting go" situation happens I actually feel lighter for the experience, calmer, and more noticeably, when I practise the letting go of events of a similar nature to the one that triggered the feeling, no longer do they affect me or if they do, it's with a much reduced charge, meaning I can let go of the energy much more easily and in turn it allows me to move forward and not get stuck.

So to encourage further understanding I have offered a way of seeing how we create ideas and thoughts to match emotions. If we now go back to the question of pain and its purpose, I want to tell you a story that helped me get a different perspective as to why we experience pain and pressure.

The lobster story

The story goes something like this. Lobsters live in the ocean. They are soft squishy-fleshed creatures but stay relatively safe from most predators, growing hard rigid shells and hiding in crevices and rocks. For the lobster the shell is a good structure to protect itself from the dangers of its environment but it does come with a drawback; unlike us humans who simply grow within their skin the lobster has a set amount of growing space in the shell and once that size is reached it must find a safe place to go through an incredible and vulnerable process of shedding its old shell so that it can form a new bigger shell to house its soft body.

The lobster actually climbs out of its old shell to grow. This is a marvel of nature to see. So how does the lobster know when it's time to shed its shell? It doesn't have a brain; it certainly won't reason what is happening and choose a course of action, so something must trigger the whole process.

For novelty's sake imagine that we were the lobster, living in a rigid shell. What might we experience as we started to run out of space within our housing? If it helps just remember for a moment when you were small and growing into and out of your shoes. They start to feel tight; the foot is squashing into the end of the shoe and we can recognise that the shoe is becoming too small for our growing foot. So like our lobster there is an experiencing of pressure, and to some degree the nervous system of the lobster may register the pressure as pain as it reaches the limit of its current shell. If the lobster had awareness, say like a human mind, what do you think it would be saying about the fact that it's feeling pressure? Would it be something like, "This is not fun, this shell is too small for me, why isn't it bigger, I don't like this, I feel like I am going to be crushed by this shell, what's wrong with me, this can't be right!"

Well as best we know, lobsters do not have human consciousness and just simply register the crossing of the threshold, a feeling of pressure/discomfort to initiate the shedding process, that process which is a mechanism for growth. The lobster just automatically lets go of the old shell in order for it to grow into its new one. To the lobster it's a natural part of the process. For humans the pain to which we refer is something we are conditioned to avoid, and for good reason. It doesn't feel good; it can range from uncomfortable to incredibly damaging, and it makes us shrink away. But I encourage you to think about it; there is benefit to be found in the experiencing of pressure and pain. Maybe we just need to stop labelling it as such in order for a greater meaning to arise from the experience.

I noticed this when observing the changing attitudes of the graduates in the sales team and how they transformed as a result of their experiences. At the time they had strong feelings about being seen to make mistakes in front of their peers, about getting it wrong or in their minds failing in some way. However, facing the experience and moving through it, they emerged with a realisation, something I too have encountered myself many times throughout my career. What they and I realised is that it's the ideas we hold that exaggerate the anxieties, pains or negative feelings rather than the experience itself. I recall coming out of a meeting I was apprehensive about, or interviews I had attended, and leaving with the sense that it wasn't half as bad as my over-active mind made it out to be.

This realisation reinforces why being present in our thoughts and not allowing the mind, unchecked, to project into the future is so important. It's not only limited to the individual. Society has a collective psyche that often exaggerates the ideas of the group it represents. Collectively there is a negative association with mistakes and so-called failure in the working environment, but as we have explored this is how we learn. When we consider the emotional aspect of that experience, the *pain*, something that is unwanted, we can see why many individually as well as collectively look upon failing and pain as we do: something negative, to be avoided and pushed down inside us.

If the lobster never let go of its old shell it would never grow, just as we must recognise that the experience of pain (and again I am talking of the emotional variety, those experiences that make our egos wince) is a means for us to go beyond that experience. If we don't we will simply stop growing. Throughout my career I have seen people who have never got past certain events. They carried the baggage of old thoughts and emotions around with them for years. In doing so it distorted their view of things they experienced and stopped them moving forward.

We call this being stuck in our ways, a label nearly only ever assigned to the older generation. For those people with years' worth of experiences building up within, it just means that they simply have not or cannot let go of whatever it is they are clinging to, or rather whatever it is that is clinging to them. They may quite possibly be unconscious as to why they respond to situations the way they do. Perhaps the sponsoring event happened long ago in the past and all they experience now is the emotional echo. When something in the external world triggers the uprising of the emotion in an attempt to release it, it's doggedly forced back down by the rigid ego and expressed as stubbornness, inflexibility or any other manifestation of the denial of the emotion.

As for the graduates we looked at in the previous chapter, whilst the real significance evaded me at the time, what I realise now is that getting it wrong, experiencing emotional pain, that feeling of being uncomfortable about making so-called mistakes, is intrinsically fundamental in growing, in becoming better in anything you or I undertake. It is the signal that we are able to grow from the experience, that it is actually an opportunity not a curse. Once overcome, whatever the underlying emotion, it is either totally cleared or significantly diminished in its strength, which means the next time it manifests it will exert a lesser force and will be easier to let go of. But to really take advantage of this opportunity to be aware of this experience and all these influences running through us there needs to be a degree of self-awareness, of consciousness of oneself, an awareness of one's own state of presence, that stillness of mind that places you in the present moment.

I can't overstate the importance of looking within and letting go, and it's something we will go into now more deeply. If you're prepared to undertake some self-analysis, looking directly at the stuff you normally stay away from due perhaps to some emotional uneasiness, embarrassment or dread surrounding those thoughts, ideas or beliefs that normally remain hidden from your conscious awareness, then limiting behaviours and their underlying causes may start to become visible. Only when you start pointing your focus in the dark corners of your mind can they be addressed.

The opportunity here is to face whatever it is you have previously shied away from, observing it directly. Accept whatever emotions may arise without judgements of yourself or previous thoughts around it, simply allowing them to play out. That is not always easy; we have a strong aversion to experiencing pain but as we touched upon in "Releasing the baggage" earlier in this chapter, the act of confronting it, letting the emotion play out, will dissipate the strength with which you hold on to it and its effect on your perceptions. Some things need more work to relinquish than others, but when you can directly observe them without the emotional charge or aversion towards them you are on the right path.

The act of letting those emotions play out, that letting go, is ultimately a lot less draining of your energy than holding on to them and living with the distortion of your perception towards related matters.

Chapter Summary

Passing through the Pain Barrier

- Things are rarely as bad as the mind makes them out to be. Don't make situations into problems.
- Painful (emotional) events can become opportunities to resolve limiting beliefs. Experience the emergent emotion without judgement or resistance. Simply try to feel the discomfort/pain without the usual accompanying mental narrative. Connect to the feeling not the story that triggered the feeling.
- Pay attention to your state. Notice when strain becomes stress.

Chapter 10 – Letting Things Go

It may be much clearer now, but I would like to further articulate why making so-called mistakes is a valuable part of the learning and growing process in everything we do and ultimately argue that there are no such things as mistakes.

Let us look at video gaming. Are you a video gamer? Maybe you know someone who is. In a previous company where I worked one of the sales team, we will call him Thomas, was just such a person, an avid gamer. He binged on game play; in fact upon the release of an eagerly anticipated game Thomas would actually take annual leave so that he could play without interruption. The latest online multiplayer adventure game would come out and he fell off the grid.

We are talking about playing for days, not hours, spending all of his free time completely consumed by the game. He is not alone. Gamers like Thomas can become completely immersed; they talk to other gamers, discussing the different aspects, the levels they got stuck on and how they overcame the obstacle that allowed them to progress. To the outsider it might appear like another world and an addictive one at that.

For this group of adventurers there is a common fact that unites them all: amongst this group not one who picks up the game from scratch ever completes every level without falter to finish in one fell swoop. It never happens but if it did it would probably be quite a disappointment.

In completing the game easily, without being tested, they would not get to experience a sense of achievement. Without a challenge there would be no sense of progression. Video games are designed to keep people playing them; they are designed with complexity to allow a stronger engagement experience, and part of that experience is crashing out of the game, so that you can pick up the controller again and keep enjoying the game. Even the crashing out is part of the enjoyment. With practice or looked upon differently, through repetition and consistency the player can experience the success of overcoming the obstacles, achieving the special level or progressing to the next stage.

Speak to any of these gamers and they will tell you how much time they put into the game. How they got stuck on a particular level and how they tried a hundred different ways to complete it. They typically played for long periods, eventually landing upon the correct sequence of moves to get them to the next stage. In doing so they encountered many approaches, each with slightly different outcomes, until they landed on the appropriate one. Therefore it was their consistency and awareness of what they tried, it was those "mistakes", the ones that didn't bring them the result they were seeking, which eventually led them to the result they wanted, the result they achieved. So were they really mistakes, or just the natural process of learning and growth?

If that analogy doesn't resonate with you sufficiently, if you are unable to see the correlation between being conscious of your actions and trying over and over again without getting bogged down with ideas of failure or pain, ultimately achieving the desired outcomes you set, then here is a challenge that almost every human being experienced, failed (by society's definition) many times and simply carried on trying until they got there...

What was it? Well, you are walking, right? As small children crawling around on all fours for a period of time we reached a transitional step in our personal development. We didn't become better at crawling; we just pulled ourselves up and tried to walk, then most likely fell down again, and then pulled ourselves up and so on, until we started to take our first steps. This process did not happen the first time we tried, and we were almost certainly helped along the way, but we just kept getting up and trying again. Why did we not give up the second, third, fourth or fifth time? What motivated us to keep trying? Well it might be in part attributed to the fact that at that stage in our experience we had no mind structure to frame the experience as a limiting belief. A sense of self did not exist because at that young age we did not have an ego. So we could not know "I am successful" or "I am failing"; we just had a desire, an imperative to get up and walk and we carried on trying until we achieved it. A lot, if not all, the limitations we encounter begin in the mind, because we have stored an idea which we make into reality.

Things change when we become older. Our sense of self, our ego, starts to form around three to four years of age. We accumulate life experience, building a substantive bank of experiential data to draw from. As salespeople when we set out to achieve a desired goal or objective, say breaking into a new account or new market, it's highly likely to varying degrees that we assess which resources may be required or maybe we don't; we might just as simply have a go without thinking on it too much! Then we either achieve it or we do not, and what happens next is the differentiator between successful and unsuccessful people. How many give up after the first, second or third attempt? The key differentiator in the consistently successful salesperson, and in fact all successful individuals, is they keep trying until they succeed, not blindly repeating the same mistakes but being conscious of their efforts and making necessary adjustments.

Look at athletes or entrepreneurs; it makes no difference which. The commonly held view is that you keep getting up every time you fall. That it is the knocks that temper one's mettle and provide experience, which develops expertise. This plays to a favourite quote by Thomas A. Edison: "I have not failed. I've just found 10,000 ways that won't work."

For the exercise completed earlier, in Chapter 7, on "getting into flow states", you were asked to list and score each of the various functions and activities of your role, such as prospecting, admin, meetings, sales meetings etc, to explore where you might be using your greatest strengths and if they correlate to those tasks most enjoyable to you.

Now, for this exercise, to understand where there might be resistance to the tasks and activities you undertake, revisit your list of activities, marking each one with either a plus or minus. The pluses being the enjoyable ones and therefore stronger aspects of your performance, and the minuses reflecting those tasks that you encounter resistance to, either prior to the commencement or as an ongoing feeling throughout their execution. For those with a minus against them, do you notice a correlation between the resistance and your sense of ability to complete competently or does it simply just not engage you? If the latter is true ask yourself what it is about the activity that you find disagreeable. We now have a clearer idea of the areas that need attention.

Starting with all the minuses or least enjoyable/least successful activities and tasks, think about each for a few minutes. What are your first thoughts towards the activity, and how does carrying out the activity make you feel? It's actually the feeling that we are looking for. Then go beyond the initial feeling by asking why – why do I feel that? Investigate if there is anything you can associate with the feeling. Do not worry if you can't. Depending on the strength of the feeling, and I make the assumption that the feeling is not a positive one, investigate further as to how you feel about the feeling. Do you wish that you didn't feel the way you do about the task?

When engaged in the task or activity, do you push the negative feeling down, out of your awareness? If you do you are not alone, and maybe you even scold yourself for the feeling. Internally saying something like "Just get over it, you've been doing this for years, you really need to get past this" or maybe it's more critical: "You really are pretty crap at this". Whatever the response, explore it. If you resist the feeling or experience of an unhelpful internal dialogue from time to time, can you say that either approach is complicit in you overcoming the obstacle? Is the mind, which gives you these responses each time you engage in the activity, really helping you overcome them to achieve your desired goal, to be better at what you do, more consistent in your improved performance, successful in the task?

Some of the most successful salespeople I have worked with had common traits that were highly likely to have contributed to the outcomes they experienced. Firstly, they were never fearful of whatever they were doing, and as strange as it sounds many salespeople have a low-level apprehension or fear towards some aspect of their role. In the teams I managed over the years calling was a fear amongst some; for others it was running senior executive level meetings. It may also point to why many sales leaders and professionals no longer see cold calling as a viable means of business development. Even if it is not the conscious reason given, it does raise a very basic fear of rejection in each of us. The level and intensity varies from person to person but it's fair to say that what distinguishes between the constantly successful and the not is that the most successful individuals will not be afraid of the call and are ok with being told no, so energetically do not carry that limiting emotion in the undercurrent of the call.

What that really means is that the level of confidence, or as I prefer self-belief, in the value that he or she brings to the sales call is much higher. When there is a greater degree of belief in oneself a more meaningful and impactful call will ensue, or any activity you engage in for that matter, because there isn't a part of your attention or energy directed in on the self, concerned with how others might see you or any other self-conscious thoughts.

You must set and regularly re-energise your intentions. It may be that you would like to have eight meaningful business meetings within your working week, that you are confident in your ability to demonstrate value during those engagements to such a degree that subsequent meetings and opportunities would ensue. Without this focus you are leaving the door wide open for your subconscious mind to play out any of the negative undercurrent emotions you may hold about the activity.

This is what I mean when I describe the conscious sale: you are being mindful of the activities, intentions and outcomes you energise. It means that you cannot act automatically or unconsciously throughout your working day, week, month or year. The conscious salesperson is the individual that focuses the considerable mental energy and resources at their disposal to the outcome of their choosing and not in default to an old idea or limiting belief.

If you feel that calling is the least enjoyable part of what you do, and that you always get the guy with little or no time for sales calls, then it's likely that's what you will be seeking for subconsciously, and then consciously experience each and every one of those matching outcomes so as to validate your subconscious belief about it. What you sought for you are mostly likely to notice, quite often at the expense of the other outcome potentialities that might manifest during the call.

As soon as you start to hear the meeting going down the route of "We are happy with our existing supplier", and "We don't see the value in moving away from our existing solution" or any negative response you've heard before, the pattern recognition part of the brain will be matching the dialogue with your underlying thoughts about it. The subconscious link will fire to that old emotion and then it becomes a self-fulfilling prophecy as you will undoubtedly feel a degree of rejection and in turn will sense your energetic state drop, and as we have covered already, the lower your state the narrower the band of perceived potentialities. You may well go through the motions, continuing to offer a case as to why your company's offering is to be further considered, but you may lack the energy of conviction.

All of what is shared here is offered on the basis that you will put these practices to the test yourself. In doing so you bring about the possibility of breaking the continuity of the patterns described above. When focused, paying attention entirely on the present moment, the probability increases of an outcome arising that is different and outside the range of your automatically triggered negative mind-driven conclusions. In short the door is open for the conversation to go in new directions, for new ideas to be shared and even if the meeting doesn't reveal any immediate opportunity to discover how you might add value to this client and their situation, that outcome arrived at through awareness creates space. That space is a discontinuity in the subconscious patterns of your mind being played out, as you stop looking to validate an old limiting idea in favour of a new potential outcome emerging.

The notion of limiting what you potentially experience was well illustrated by a business mentor some years ago when we did a little exercise in his office. Within a 10 second period I was to count as many items in the room that were red as I could. When the clock started I quickly scanned the room, totalling up all the red items in the room. I think it was something like 12 things. When the clock stopped he asked if I had the number in mind, and I replied that I did. He then asked me how many items in the room were blue.

We see and experience things that we filter for, so if there are old memories and emotions stored in the background of your mind, in the absence of newer, stronger positive intentions, we will default to the old and likely negative ideas which when actively played out become intentions.

So setting your intentions suddenly becomes a lot more relevant. If you want to enable yourself with the best tools then set strong intentions.

Chapter Summary

Letting Things Go

- Awareness is the foundation of change. Take action now by making a list, noting down each aspect of your role you like and dislike.
- Against each, mark with a plus or minus then examine each of the negatively marked activities, spending a few minutes exploring what your feelings are towards the activity.
- Make a note of those feelings and then go beyond them by asking "why" of those feelings: "Why do I feel that way?"
- Try to articulate that reason, and then ask again why it is you feel that way, continuing until you get to a point where you cannot resolve the feeling to a cause any further.

- What you arrive at is the sponsoring feeling/event that underpins all the other thought patterns at play. Addressing that will undoubtedly move you away from the old paradigm and will facilitate a change of attitude towards your engagement with whatever it was you had resistance towards.
- For this exercise to be beneficial you must be entirely honest with your answers. That honesty may be uncomfortable but your perseverance will be rewarded with awareness that may have previously been hidden.

Chapter 11 – Setting Intentions

In which areas of our working day would we benefit from setting intentions? All of them, all the parts of our day where we engage with an activity or task where we have a desired outcome that can be enhanced by setting a conscious intention. These are not only the gross aspects of the sale, the milestones such as qualification, solutioning, presenting etc. It's applicable for data entry, number crunching and the researching of a prospective client. Setting intentions helps frame in the mind what it is we are seeking to accomplish. As I have said before, it creates a map for the mind and subconscious mind to drive towards.

Setting intentions prior to making calls

Cold calling is a function of sales, especially if you are within the new business element of the sales environment. So what is our intention? We must be clear on what it is we are looking to achieve. Calling becomes this continuous stream of activity that is most likely undertaken unconsciously, meaning do we really stop and set our intentions?

So start your new practice, assuming that you have set your positive state, that's to say you have energised yourself through exercise, music or other methods, and that you come to the cold calling activity having prepared all your material, the people you are calling, names, numbers etcetera.

Then set your intentions, and when setting those intentions include the desired outcome of each call: the desired outcome on the number of positive conversations, that is strong business conversations, and the number of appointments booked.

Essentially you need to determine and visualise the outcome that you would like for each facet of the sales process. From my experience when cold calling in to new businesses I would often decide that I would make 50 phone calls that day, and of those 50 phone calls it would be my intention to have at least 15 strong business conversations that led to five meetings. The more detail you go into with the visualisation and the intention setting, the more likely it is you're going to experience it.

Also when visualising the desired outcome, imagine what shape and form your ideal client might take, and then ask yourself if you reflect those qualities and energy. We attract who we are. Look at your friends and associates; there will be aspects of them that reflect you and your values, so it is likely you will energetically draw those kinds of personality to you.

If you are one of those people who finds cold calling the least enjoyable aspect of your role then choose to set the intention on the outcome of the conversation based on the kind of person you're looking to speak with. What does that mean? For example, you might say "It is my intention to have 10 excellent quality business conversations with receptive IT managers."

Whatever you might have experienced in terms of negative outcomes from your calling sessions – it might be you encounter a lack of receptivity to your calls, perhaps people are frustrated that you called them, maybe they are rude, or don't have time to take your call – start by setting an intention that is counter to the experiences that have previously been running.

If you want to have meaningful conversations that lead to meetings, that must be the focus of the intention you set. The failure to set a strong positive outcome intention will result in you defaulting to the strongest emotional experience that is running in your subconscious. If your sales cold calling experience is of people hanging up on you, set an opposite intention, one that states you're going to have at least 20 people answer the phone and of those 20 people 10 of them will be called at the perfect time to discuss a new project they are working on.

With any discipline you must practise, so doing this once will not likely bring about the desired change, especially if you are still holding elements of doubt about the efficacy of this approach. I urge you to practise this approach daily, and you must commit to this practice consistently for at least one month. If you want to rewrite the underlying programming in your subconscious which has governed your experiences potentially for many years, that is to say the emotional undercurrent that you are unaware of that plays out as negative experiences when you have these calls, then you need to implant a stronger thought, backed up with the belief.

Setting intentions for meetings

Just as we set intentions for a call we must set intentions for our meetings. What is it that we are seeking to achieve? Be specific in your mind as to what you want to get out of that meeting and then energise that intention. Do this by placing yourself into a calm state as we did before, ensuring that the intention is always set when you are in a high state and never ever setting an intention when you are feeling down or feeling negative, because you will only attract an outcome to match that energy.

Remember that energy attracts like energy so if you set your intention in a high state you would likely attract the high state outcome. Be clear and specific. It sometimes helps just to make a note of what it is you wish to achieve. For an experienced salesperson it is very easy to get to a point in your career when you consider that you know what you are doing and continue to work almost in an autopilot state when performing certain aspects of the role. You've conducted a great many meetings and you know what you want from them but sometimes it's good just to stop and take perspective on what it is that you do.

Act then evaluate – that is an important function of being successful. As salespeople we need to understand what makes us successful. This is one of the principles of all prominent sales programmes – what made us successful yesterday isn't necessarily going to make us successful today and therefore we need to know why we have experienced success.

This consideration is typically appropriate to the "doing" aspect of the job but it is also applicable to the non-actionable, intangible aspects of what we do, that is to say the way that we approach topics, tasks and activities mentally before we undertake them.

Therefore, we must visualise our intent. We must be clear on what it is that we want to communicate. We must be clear on what it is that we want to achieve and then set that as the intention, remembering that failing to set a strong intention defaults to the underlying emotional current. You may not have a strong negative aversion to a particular aspect and therefore your meeting will run according to the energy that you bring to it but the effectiveness of that meeting, like the effectiveness of anything you undertake, always increases when you set an intention.

The old adage that if you aim at nothing, you will hit it, applies. If you focus your attention, the more detail you give to that focus, the more appropriate the outcome will be in terms of matching the desired outcome when you set an intention. It will serve you then if you set the intention that you will meet with the type of person that you want to speak to, that you will be able to communicate succinctly your value proposition, that they will be receptive to this and that you will achieve whatever it is that you are looking to achieve as an outcome of that meeting.

It is that straightforward; there is no magic here. It is simply that if you approach the task with clearly defined objectives set as an intention you are more likely to achieve your goal and this is reflected by professional athletes and captains of industry all over. Ask any successful athlete or entrepreneur and they will tell you that without setting the belief, intention and state you are almost guaranteed to fail. Every athlete is going out there with the intention of winning or improving on their time, beating their personal best. The sales environment is no different: you need to set a winning intention and you need to state to yourself what it is you will achieve.

The greater the clarity the more likelihood there is of you meeting that intention.

Setting intentions for sales presentations

The sales presentation is an intrinsic part of any salesperson's activity. It might be for delivering the initial engagement value proposition or it might be to present the final solution. Setting the right intention for the outcome of this meeting is incredibly important; in fact it is critical.

Setting an intention works in parallel with the "doing" preparation you might already undertake when composing your presentation. That "doing" preparation includes articulating what it is you wish to convey and to whom. If the audience is made up of several people they may each have their own set of buying criteria. Identifying their role within the meeting should already have been undertaken.

We must set the intention to focus on communicating the appropriate salient points to each individual member of the audience. In order to do this we must be clear on what we are setting out to achieve and on what the key objectives of this meeting are.

We undertake the same practice as for the intention setting. Ideally the night before the meeting, get yourself into a high state: listen to music or prior to this go for a run, anything that energises you, then sit down and take several conscious breaths, focusing on your breathing. When your mind is still, set out the intention for the meeting tomorrow. Visualise the details of the meeting: see the travelling to the meeting as a hassle-free part of the process, with you arriving in plenty of time. See what it is you wish to achieve and communicate. Imagine what the meeting participants will understand and take away from the meeting. Be granular; spend three or four minutes doing this. The bigger the meeting the greater the value in visualising more detail. Once you've done that then let it go; you have set an energised intention.

I will make it clear, though, that for any salesperson, having carried out the basics before this point is a given. That is to say, you know your products and services inside out (there is no excuse for not knowing this) and how they solve your client's big problem. Secondly, you must know your market environment. When working within a particular market vertical it is essential that you understand not only the circumstances for the company you are approaching or working with, but also the industry-wide topics that are being considered and tackled by the market participants.

You have to be a market expert able to add value to the call, meeting or proposal. It's no longer about selling your services or products to a company that needs them. A successful salesperson must be able to perfectly and succinctly articulate a value proposition that communicates a disproportionate amount of value to the intended audience; whether that is in monetary terms or consultative expertise brought to the conversation, you cannot rely on being a nice guy for the customer account or the falsely positive caller prospecting the new company. You have to know your value and the value you represent to the client, then when you set the intended outcome you have quality content to underpin your self-belief, and energetically that will resonate louder than from anyone that does not cover these areas.

Self-belief is the currency of performance, and with it you can buy yourself a greater slice of the opportunities you discover.

Chapter Summary

Setting Intentions

- Arriving at the conclusion of this section, I ask you to apply what you have learnt but before you do I would make a suggestion, a request which I have not come across in other books. I am writing this because of something my mentor once said: "Reading a book once doesn't mean you know what it stands for." Go back and reread this entire section. Why? Because for me every book that I have been inspired by, those that have spoken to me, whether it be career developmental, philosophical or fictional, I have discovered deeper levels of insight and appreciation with every subsequent reading. I am saying that as I broadened my awareness it enabled a greater dimension of understanding to arise.

- If your energetic state is the foundation of all that we explore together, then the understanding of the mind and setting of intentions are the mechanics to achieving the success you seek. That is not to suggest that in reading this book again you will have a life changing revelation, but do not rule it out. Some of the simplest texts I have read have had the most profound effects on the way I look at things. So go back and reread this section. You might just see things differently, with greater appreciation the second time around.

Part 4 – Belief

Chapter 12 – What Do You Believe?

You can have anything you want if you are willing to give up the belief that you can't have it.

In the last section I encouraged you to examine the ways in which you might end up far from your desired destination as a consequence of not setting a strong intention. I have sought to illustrate in this simple approach to setting strong empowering intentions what happens in the absence of that practice. We have examined the role in which memory formation in our past and our subconscious association with it can distort the way in which we perceive the events unfolding around us in the present moment, and have considered how the subconscious mind attempts to release mental and emotional baggage collected over the years through the process of letting go.

We have looked at how the conscious aspect of the mind can easily misidentify, letting go only to subvert the process in order to make sense of a distorted perception of reality. I encourage you to practise letting go and identify the behavioural patterns and changes to the way you engage with your activities which can leave space for a new dimension of experience and interpretation. That space permits the perception of events differently. In doing so, you may start to see painful events as opportunistic ones rather than being simply bad, as well as how our attachment to the way we think things should happen can also limit our ability to maximise our potential in any given situation.

Now revisiting the three Points of Conscious Performance, following from state and intention comes belief. Belief is equally as important as setting your intention and putting yourself into a higher state. In fact belief is everything; without it you are making a subconscious statement that you do not expect to succeed in whatever it is you set out to do. You may have set intentions but without belief they will not come to fruition. Belief is essential to keep you on the path to reach your objectives, because without it as soon as the road becomes rocky, when the task seems more difficult than you first imagined, you would probably encounter the idea of giving up. You might not have the luxury of actually having the option to give up, but the idea or a form of it will enter your mind. If you are the type of person that struggles to hold the belief that something is possible I suggest you start with small steps. Do not believe that you can make your year's target in one day because it's not likely to happen.

However start by believing in your ability to achieve smaller things and scale up. Be consistent in your belief and achievement of those things. Doing so reinforces the achievement of those intentions that you set and the belief that supported it; it is like building up a credit in the mind's bank of possibility. The more familiar you become with the experience of meeting your objectives, the more familiar you become with experiencing the success of those achievements and the more belief in your ability feels natural and congruent to the objectives that you set. From the highest state we place ourselves in, we are set to declare our intentions. We then have a choice: do we fully commit to those intentions through total belief in our intended outcome or do we entertain doubt? In the sales environment what you believe in will ultimately shape your sales experience; in fact this is true throughout life, so the question is, do you choose enabling beliefs?

For many the notion of belief is simple: you either believe in something or you do not, but not believing in something can actually be the same thing. The stronger you energise an idea with focus and attention over time the more likely it is to become a belief. So in the sales environment, what are your prevailing beliefs?

My experience has confirmed Henry Ford's famous quote: "Whether you think you can, or you think you can't – you're right."

Based upon my years of experience working with a multitude of salespeople, exhibiting a broad spectrum of ability, achievement and personal belief, to me there appear to be just two mindsets that sales professionals may fall within. Those that believe "I can" and those that believe "I can't". This of course is not a conscious choosing or an awareness, but more to the observer a recognisable behavioural pattern that reflects the mindset of the individual through the ways in which they respond to situations and events taking place around them.

The irony of this is that both positions, those two mindsets, require belief to maintain them; it is just that the negative form is not clearly recognised as belief in the way in which we view positive belief. It's almost unconscious. If we examine the reality around the two ideas we realise that regardless of which, we must consciously reinforce the idea we believe in frequently so that it holds steadfast until such time as it is adopted as fact planted firmly in our subconscious. It follows then that the prevailing belief you energise will engage your subconscious mind to bring you the reality of the belief.

Every single person believes in something: they do, you do, and it is a fact. That you know you believe in something is an entirely different matter. Under-the-hood thinking accounts for almost all of our mental cognitive processing. A staggering 95% of our brain activity, in terms of cognition, is activity beyond our conscious awareness. Only 5% of our mental constructs, thought processes and reasoning are done at a conscious level. Most of your life is actually experienced on a kind of autopilot, with the subconscious mind doing most of the information processing and making available to the conscious mind a filtered set of data to interpret so that you can make sense of the world around you. That thin slice of reality is essential to avoid sensory overload, to allow you to understand and deal with what is happening in that moment.

So given the magnitude of the hidden processing within the subconscious mind it becomes less surprising when introduced to the notion that ideas and beliefs about ourselves are formed and held in the deeper unknown part of our mind. Ideas about our capabilities, what we should earn, what we can and cannot achieve; they are all rooted in the subconscious where they reside to frame our conscious awareness and sense of possibility.

Now would be a good time to take a few moments to ask, "What do I believe in?" If you are already a person of faith, whether that be in religion, your football team or the weather's endless capacity to rain on the day you want a BBQ, then the good news is you are already halfway there. You are because you already believe in something, so the mechanics of conscious belief are firmly established within your psyche. However if you find yourself scratching your head, thinking that faith, belief, whatever you term it is irrational, let us start with a simple question and explore the meaning.

Taking a strictly left-brained, that is to say, logical approach to the concept, let me position belief as being simply an energetic value, that is, the amount of mental energy we put into an idea without there being empirical evidence to prove it to be true. Alternatively if you prefer it could be viewed as to be saying it is a mental position, one that represents an attitude positively (or negatively) orientated towards the likelihood of something being true.

To explore further we start with the first description, that belief is an energetic value we place on an idea. Therefore, belief would have started out as a thought, an idea about something. Then at what point does the thought we have stop being just a thought and become something stronger? When does it become a belief? Moreover, is a belief strengthened by other actions, things that we observe external to us, external to the thought form we hold in our mind? Can these ideas be strengthened through certain behaviours? Can speaking your ideas out loud, as in a declaration to yourself or others, reinforce the meaning and strength to you? Yes they can.

Furthermore, if your actions as well as your words and thoughts were to become congruent with the outcome of the belief, those actions would increase the likelihood of the outcome matching the belief. If you were to start acting as if the outcome was assured and entertain no other potentiality, do you think you would have a lesser or greater likelihood of achieving the objective?

There are many questions posed there and although I have offered some answers, please take a moment and investigate for yourself. I have summarised them again below. Please give extra thought around the last one. Investigate within to see if there have been times in your life when you achieved something that at first seemed out of your reach but at some point your energy towards it shifted and you believed you could do it and indeed did achieve it.

- When do your thoughts become beliefs?
- Can your ideas be strengthened through you undertaking certain behaviours?
- Can speaking your ideas out loud, as in a declaration to yourself or others, reinforce the meaning and strength to you?
- If you were to start acting as if the outcome is assured and entertain no other potentiality, do you think you have a lesser or greater likelihood of achieving the objective?

Now put the book down and consider the questions, letting each one linger for a moment and then making notes about each answer you arrive at.

Ok, what came up for you? Your answers are your answers; what came up if you thought about each question, letting the question just sit there in your mind, is likely to be a reflection of what's held under the hood.

Evidence of belief and the athlete

You really do not have to look that far to see evidence of the power of belief. Evidence is abundant, especially in the arena of professional sports. To the professional athlete belief is the difference between taking the gold and silver medal.

The strength of your belief will affect the outcome of your goals; how much is down to the individual. To the sales professional, self-belief is the currency of performance as it is for the athlete. If you do not think so consider the Olympic gold medal winner and ask yourself, is there a consistency of thought, word and action within that person? Is that not belief manifested? They do what they do because they believe they will succeed, but which comes first? Belief or the congruence of their thoughts, words and actions?

It seems somewhat ironic that society as a whole accepts belief is a requisite trait for the athlete and must be present for their success to be realised. Most people are fully accepting of the high level of commitment, focus and determination that the athlete must commit to in order to reach their potential. That commitment is essential for them to achieve the levels of performance needed to be a gold medal winner. To reach those levels of performance you must have strength of mind, and laser focus to ensure the training, diet and mindset disciplines are all maintained. Most of all the athlete continues to believe, actually *must* believe, that the attainment of their winning/success intention is entirely possible. The irony for me is why we think it should it be any different for the salesperson, or any other profession to achieve and experience those upper levels of performance. After all, that's why you have come to this material: you are reading this book because you want to achieve something you feel you currently have yet to reach or experience.

For some of you reading this, you will be thinking that it is easier said than done, that belief is demanding of one's energy and that energy starts to wane after time. To those of you, I agree; it can be. When writing the last section many questions came up for me; they were all entirely relevant and they need to be given expression too so that you can find the answers for the questions that follow for yourself, and we will address them shortly. But to revisit the idea that maintaining belief is energy draining, let us explore that further.

Research for this book led me to different sports psychologists' views of the relationship of belief and the motivation to succeed: the notion that motivation to succeed in your chosen activity is a key part of maintaining belief in the attainment of your goals. Whilst I agree with the vast majority of the commentators within this area on the premise that the way you think ultimately affects how you perform, I feel a distinction is needed when we speak of motivation.

Within the sports science and academic community motivation has been distilled down into two aspects, *extrinsic* and *intrinsic* motivation. Extrinsic motivation is looked upon as the drive underpinning the performance of an activity to attain a desired outcome.[12] It is theorised that the drive to act when we refer to extrinsic motivation emanates from influences beyond oneself. Common extrinsic motivations are rewards like the pursuit of money, such as a promotion at work or to gain favour with a client. That said, it can also be a response to negative stimulus including the threat of punishment following indiscretion, insubordination or another instance where an undesired outcome is navigated around through specific actions being taken to ensure the avoidance of the unwanted outcome. In the area of sports, competition is seen as an extrinsic motivator because it encourages the performer to win and to beat others. A cheering crowd and the desire to win a trophy are extrinsic incentives,[13] similar to the desire to beat a rival company in a bid or pursue a sales award. In short, look at extrinsic motivation as a battery, and like all batteries eventually the power runs down and it requires a recharge. This idea is fine if the vessel being motivated (that is, you) is indeed rechargeable. Not all batteries are, and certainly not without being plugged into an external power supply.

Not all goals and targets you set or which are set for you are sufficient to overcome the resistance to re-energise your motivation once it has drained down. Maybe what moved you to action was the rousing speech from the sales director at the beginning of the quarter, but now you are absent of that external energy (power supply) you may well find it difficult to find the enthusiasm for the task you have ahead of you.

---

[12] https://en.wikipedia.org/wiki/Motivation#cite_note-Ryan.2C_R._M._2000-5

[13] https://en.wikipedia.org/wiki/Motivation#cite_note-Motivation-12

So if extrinsic drive is a battery charge that slowly or quickly depletes over time then intrinsic motivation is the dynamo that is a self-perpetuating source of energy orientated to achieving whatever you set out to achieve. Whereas extrinsic motivation emanates from an external source, the power of intrinsic motivation comes from a place within. To me this echoes my understanding of inspiration and for the purposes of this book I will continue from here on the basis that when we discuss motivation it is of the extrinsic type and inspiration represents motivation of an intrinsic type.

Why? Because I believe that as a starting point when we speak of inspiration each of you will be much closer to an understanding of what I am seeking to convey through your own experience. For most within the sales environment it is likely that you have experience of inspirational leaders. My inspiration came from a sales director early on in my career who emitted an energy which sparked within me a desire to be the best I could be, to excel in what I set about. Who inspired you when you were setting out? Perhaps it was your first sales manager who sparked within you a desire to achieve something less tangible than money or praise but which had more depth and meaning? Someone who instilled in you a sense of something, dare it be said, trite as it may sound, something nobler than the pursuit of money, such as the idea of being the best sales professional you could be for the sake of it alone?

So what of inspiration? When were you last inspired to achieve something, and again I mean for the simple honest pleasure of doing something unselfish, not for the pat on the back, not for what you can get materially, maybe so that you can give something back? How does being in that "spirit" differ from being motivated in your experience?

Experience has led me to "believe" that being in spirit with what you are engaged in is in part the same as finding "flow" with what you do. Going back to the battery analogy for a moment, motivation does indeed give you the jolt to launch you into action. That sales incentive, the pressure of the quarters target, the friendly but real competition amongst your peers within the company, they are all excellent and the battery charge is sufficient to keep you on track, for the day, the week, but how about the month? And what about quarter after quarter? When all the banter, hype and noise subsides it comes down to a simple fact, that it is you that needs to find the energy to stay the distance, not to drop the pace, or lose the focus, without entertaining doubt that your goals are achievable. As time passes, for those that call upon external sources for their why, without continued re-energising of that why (new motivations), if what you do is not completely aligned with your set intentions and underpinned by a strong inner sense of why, that thing that inspires you to reach higher, the burden of your underlying doubt can easily outweigh your motivations. Especially like our battery, the charge from which you sprung to action starts to dissipate, and in short you stop believing you can and start to give energy to the belief you might not.

What does belief look like?

If we are to better understand belief we must examine it from all sides, not just from our own perspective. To that end I ask you to consider, what does a strong belief in one's ability actually look like to the external world, to your peers, your clients, to your managers? What traits, behaviours or attitudes indicate strong self-belief?

In the sales environment belief is often expressed as confidence, which is a natural consequence of strong self-belief. When you are confident it is also true that positivity far more easily follows. So does belief look like confidence and therefore reflect a constant positive demeanour regardless of the situation?

It is a good question, because you might reasonably conclude that constant positivity is synonymous with strong self-belief, and that is not surprising because the exterior perspective of both behaviour types looks very similar. The way you consistently present yourself to the world has as much influence on your inner self as your inner self has on the way you present yourself. Over time whichever is prevalent, inner thoughts or conscious actions and behaviours, will ultimately prevail. What I am saying is that the inner beliefs within the subconscious, including those limiting beliefs we harbour consciously or otherwise, can indeed impact the way we interact in and are seen by those in our environment, as we examined in the previous section.

As part of the process of overwriting a limiting belief, we must change our body language, our thoughts and our words. In doing so they start to supplant the old ideas, if the new conscious behaviour is different to the subconsciously held belief. If it is the same then you will start to accelerate the realisation of what you seek to achieve, because there is an alignment inside and out. However, please let us be clear, that is not to say you must be falsely positively towards everything. It is not natural to be happy about a deal that is lost, the customer service issue that gets logged, or even the flat tyre on the way home. You are not being authentic if you paint a false smile on your face saying it does not matter or that everything is good when it is not. That does not serve anyone. To those around you it looks false and for you it just burns through the available energy you have which inhibits you energising more beneficial ideas as you are fundamentally denying the reality of the situation.

In the face of those situations, the approach that I have come to see as the cleanest way to move past it, as described before in Chapter 6, is simply not to label it and offer no inner resistance to it. Just acknowledge the situation for what it is dispassionately; do not moan and do not pretend it does not matter. Being neutral does not mean you have to be happy about the situation. It means you recognise it for what it is. Be positive in what you do to resolve issues that arise; be positively orientated to what you set out to achieve but be wary of anyone that is always highly positive. Consider the old saying that the light that burns twice as bright burns half as long.

The question is, how does the person with strong self-belief differ from a person who is always positive? The person that believes strongly in their ability or the outcomes of their endeavours will undoubtedly demonstrate a deep level of confidence, and of course when we are confident about something we reflect this from our energetic state, which to the exterior world can be seen as a positive attitude directed towards our targeted goal.

However the person quietly believing in their desired outcome is not by definition the person that is always overly positive. In fact being continually positive can be as restrictive as someone that is negative in his or her demeanour. They are both polar opposites of a mindset and those polarities take a lot of mental energy to maintain, energy that would be better directed to productive and creative ends rather than maintaining a false mindset about what you think you are rather than just getting on with being who you are.

We live in a relative universe, and that relativity, that is to say the relationship each and every thing has, is predicated on the simple but universal fact that it is what it is in relation to what it is not. I can know hot because I have experience of cold, left from right, fast from slow, right? You know the opposites or are at least aware of them. So in order to be constantly positive it means you have experienced or are aware of the opposite of being always positive; you know what it is because you see what it is not. To maintain the position of constant positivity requires a lot of effort. If you are operating at an extreme mental position then it is entirely possible that, if and when the requisite energy currently maintaining that mental position no longer has sufficient charge to hold it, the individual will experience the counter position of their energetic state: the very low state. You were up, then energy drops; you will then likely experience the down. For how long is entirely down to the individual and their circumstances. To help position it another way we can use an analogy that may help further, so let us consider the pendulum.

Science has shown us that to hold the pendulum bob, the weight at the end of the string, at a position of 30 degrees, an amount of constant energy is required. Without a force holding the bob in place it swings away from that 30 degrees position. In fact if you move a pendulum to 30 degrees and release it, it moves through its swing with a force placing it at the equal and opposite end of the oscillation, –30 degrees. It is a counter position of the starting point. So to occupy any position within the range of motion the oscillation of the pendulum requires energy and always results in the movement to the equal and opposite position. With the exception of one point in the movement: there is one position the pendulum can be at without the need of energy to be expended to maintain that position. If you release the pendulum bob from 30 degrees it will swing until the forces at work cancel themselves out and as such with each oscillation the position reached is reduced until the pendulum bob comes to rest at the equilibrium point. Simply put, if you find the balance between two extremes you find the path of least resistance and in that space being is effortless.

You might be asking, what does all this have to do with belief and why am I making this distinction? I am making this distinction because I want you to understand that your inner belief does not require you to convince the world of that conviction by maintaining a shiny positive exterior towards everything in your working life. The strength of the inner belief is that you know the belief is tangible, that you do not need to create an exterior persona to reinforce your convictions. Just moving and acting with the strength of purpose underpinned by your belief in what you do will be evident to all around you. It reminds me of a quote by Ralph Waldo Emerson, "What you do speaks so loudly that I cannot hear what you say."

As we started with the athlete as an example we will continue with that theme. As stated, it is widely accepted that they must have a success-based mindset, that is, the belief and strength of mind to achieve their desired outcomes, agreed? Good. The truth is Olympic class athletes are not born with gold medal winning capabilities immediately accessible to them. They most likely had a natural talent and a love of distance running, sprinting, or swimming etc.

That natural talent was simply an indicator for them, identifying their potential more clearly and certainly, for those that foster talent, it would be immediately recognisable as potential. Nevertheless, let us be clear that when Mo Farah, Usain Bolt or Michael Phelps were small children it was not a realised outcome that they would one day achieve the results they have. They simply had a natural ability, an indicator of potential. Jump forward a number of years and the contender Olympians are all in regular training in pursuit of their set intentions, their beliefs that they could take gold.

In order to qualify for the 2016 summer games, a male runner of the 5000 metres had to achieve a qualifying time of 13 minutes 25 seconds. If their current time is 14 minutes 10 seconds that athlete does not just keep practising the distances repetitively in the hope that just his effort alone will make the difference up. That athlete, working with their coach, will look at every aspect of their performance, break the race down into the constituent parts, the start, does the athlete get a good spring off the blocks, is the timing split second perfect to leave the start line at the optimum moment?

They will examine the pace at each stage of the race, identifying where the pace potential needs to be adjusted to maintain the best ratio of speed and energy available to make the distance at a winning time. They will examine the finish; the athletes start to push themselves at the right time, drawing on all their physical and mental strength to coincide the finish with the expenditure of all their energy. The diet will be examined: does it fuel the body accordingly to provide the desired level of fitness? The athlete's psychology will be examined: does the self-talk, the voice given to their ideas, thoughts and beliefs provide positive enabling messages that translate into a winning mentality?

All of those things, each and every one of those aspects, reinforce the likelihood of a desired outcome. It should not come as a surprise then that when you align the best thinking with the best practice/training available you can bring about the outcome of success. Such that it would be a natural consequence to believe your ability was sufficient to achieve your goals, and your words and actions become congruent with what you wish to achieve and in doing so the belief is a consequence of your mental orientation towards the likelihood of the desired outcome.

Belief becomes natural because you are behaving in a manner consistent with the success you seek. That is belief. That faith in your training is the truth of the matter, that you have given 100% to the attainment of your goals, that you listened without ego or resistance to your coach accepting that they see the potential of what you can achieve, and laid down a path for you to follow to access it. If you behaved that way with your sales career, if you aligned your thoughts and actions with a success-based paradigm, would you believe you could achieve consistent success? Perhaps, however, you struggle to hold the belief because you know honestly that you do not train like an Olympian, that you do not approach your work with the focus and dedication required, which is why your mind sabotages your efforts and your motivation drains when the reality of what you do rather than who you are is examined and found to be wanting.

That is a hard one to swallow, well it was for me, so think about it for a while, and do not read any further for now. Just consider if you ever doubt your ability to earn more, achieve more sales, or climb the corporate ladder. Does that doubt arise because you judge what you do to be less than required, not enough?

Is it really that you fear your success?

"Our deepest fear is not that we are inadequate. Our deepest fear is that we are powerful beyond measure."

Those lines are from Marianne Williamson's popular poem. When I first encountered that poem, I could not articulate why but somehow the words spoke to me. I have reread it many times but all the while I took something from it I did not know what that was. Then some time later a mentor quoted it to me and he asked whether the blockage to further success for most people was because of a fear of being successful.

That question and what it implied was crazy. Why would anyone fear success? I didn't; I knew that. I looked back across my career, the money I had earned, the positions attained, the responsibility and all that went with it, and I just could not find any evidence of a fear of that success. I even asked other salespeople on similar journeys if they feared success or if it had inhibited them in any way. Despite exploring the question it just hung there, unanswered. It remained unanswered for a long time.

Then some months before the decision to write this book the question came back. I started to think again about how I felt about previous events and opportunities throughout my sales journey, those milestones that in hindsight punctuated significant changes and directions in my career. I started to think about the job changes, the transitions from salesperson to sales manager, and I looked at the evaluation process I went through before accepting the role. You see, I had doubts about accepting my first sales manager role, but at that time it wasn't a fear of success that made me question whether I really wanted the responsibility of a team; I absolutely wanted to earn more money, build my reputation, develop my abilities. No, it was something else.

Then in a moment of clarity I had a realisation that the question of whether people are fearful towards success was the wrong question. It is not that some people block their potential through a fear of success. Reflecting on my own career, the question of the role was about whether I could actually do it and be "successful". Taking a side-by-side comparison of the two roles, my current situation was I was a known quantity, I was successful, closing deals, earning good money, I had the respect of my peers and most importantly I was comfortable with the work I did for what I got in return. On the other hand, the new role was different. I may have been approached but I knew that it would mean starting again from scratch, proving myself, my ability and of course being taken out of my comfort zone by taking on a new role full of unknowns.

The real question, the one that had been elusive, was "Do people block their potential for success through a fear that it demands massive change?" I have come to see that the apprehension towards the role was really a blanket feeling that covered more than just self-doubt. At some deeper level I knew I would be expected to deliver greater than I delivered at that time. That increase in performance would mean change, change in every aspect of what I was doing. I sensed it would mean less time for myself and making difficult decisions, some of which would not be popular with everyone, and that was a challenge for me.

And whilst those thoughts about it may not have been clearly articulated at the forefront of my awareness, as I reflect, it becomes clear that the general feeling of uncertainty towards the role was exactly the fear of what it would mean if I were to choose the path of success and growth. Nothing stays the same and if you want to develop anything beyond where it currently stands there will be change. Just like the lobster story in the previous section, growth means change, and it's our attitude towards change which can influence the outcome being experienced as either something beneficial or as something we resist and create inner conflict against.

See for yourself the change you have undertaken from your first job. See how the targets have increased, how your daily activities have developed and changed, the level of responsibility you hold to your business for accurate reporting and responsible contract writing; all these aspects are likely to be a great distance from where you set out in your sales career.

As we get older, without self-exploration we become more certain, that is to say rigid, about whom we think we are. What is possible and what is not is far more easily defined at 45 than 25. Why is that?

Let us go back to the Olympian. At some point the budding athlete was faced with what was probably a massive choice, and that choice was a fork in the road of their life's journey. And depending on what choice they made they would be set on a specific path. Somewhere in the athlete's past they had to ask if they had the discipline, the clarity of mind and the determination to consistently choose between what they wanted in that present moment of now and what they wanted most of all: settling for what they could have today or daring to dream big and pursue it intensely.

In those early days of our sales careers we are more plastic in our thinking; we are more likely to form and more easily re-form ideas about the environment and ourselves and of course what we can accomplish. We may not know what the future holds but we know it's bigger and brighter than it is now, and we have to varying degrees belief that we'll achieve more than we currently have. So what happened? Do you find yourself with the experiences you had dreamed of? Has your career led to where you hoped it would, believed it would? Actually how many of you recognised the point in your life where you had that choice presented to you? No, you don't recall; it did not happen? You never saw yourself as an athlete in training for the big challenges? Do not worry if you didn't. I really don't think very many people do.

Let us step back to the beginning of this section and examine further the idea that our subconscious thinking actually forms the structural boundaries in which we frame our sense of what is possible for us. Ever noticed how some people just cannot seem to get on an even keel (maybe you experience this yourself), how all efforts go into prospecting, building up the pipeline to have a great quarter, only to follow with a bad one? Up and down the performance goes, never consistent. Why is that?

As a sales manager I would be quick to identify inconsistent activity, taking the foot off the gas in respect to prospecting during the closing months. We all know that today's inactivity is paid for next quarter, but why is that? If it were impossible to balance both then there would be consistency in the inconsistency of sales performance, but we know that not to be the case; the 20% doing 80% of sales are consistent, so it comes back down to mindset.

It's how they think that differs and in the opening section of the book I illustrated the differing attitudes which distinguish between salespeople, BUT the mindset differences are very much conscious decisions on how to act, engage and what they seek to achieve and it is quite likely that there is an alignment of inner beliefs and outer intentions. Whereas in this context, in the case of our inconsistent salesperson, it is indeed possible that the inner limiting beliefs of what they are worth in terms of salary, how much they can earn in respect of commissions and all the other value judgements one might in the real world seek to better themselves against, are not in alignment. That they say and do one thing but think something entirely different, or at least subconsciously hold the idea/belief of a contrary position, is where we can start to see patterns and get a sense of why that is the case.

The simple answer is that to achieve things of consequence, so that we might stand out as a reflection of who we are, there must be an alignment with your thinking. In fact your thoughts beget your words and they precede your actions, and all must align for the creative forces of the subconscious mind to manifest the experiences you intended.

Although this section is entitled "Belief", it is closer to the truth that it is really about what inspires you. There is a close connection between belief and inspiration in the way they fuel action and tenacity, especially in the face of difficulty. Most of what we do is a drive to secure the basic needs such as shelter, food and security. Once those needs are met we can invest more resources in the form of time and energy to pursue things beyond those basics.

The enjoyment of the activity and becoming better today than you were yesterday is actually a great reward in itself. I have always looked at work situations like this: if I ever stopped waking up wanting to go to work to do the job that I had chosen every day for a month then I would know that I was ready for a change. I have never really understood colleagues that complained about the job continuously. I'm not saying I have never had off days but my principal default state was to be accepting and enjoying what I had chosen to do, because we all choose to work where we work. We have the choice to seek an alternate role if we find ourselves at odds with the pay plan, the competition for what we sell, or the company direction and management. No one is holding a gun to your head saying you must suffer the role.

Belief gives you the energy to continue in the face of what might be difficult. Belief is easy to profess when everything appears to be going your way, but it's most needed when the path becomes tougher and the goal less clear on the horizon. A salesman that doesn't believe, that doesn't have faith in themself, someone who relies entirely on the external motivations, may end up working harder as they have to overcome not only the real world challenges of competition but also the internal battle with their own ego.

When you are centred in your own beingness, when you come from an alignment of raised state, and set intention and empowering belief as to what you are able to achieve, you are far more powerful and resilient. You are less likely to give energy to the egoic ideas that arise from the old limiting beliefs that something is too hard, or that the task at hand is bigger than you are. When you come from that centred place you start to move into a new paradigm of being, that of being of successful in what you do.

Chapter Summary

- Belief in your desired outcomes is enhanced through the alignment of your thoughts, words and actions. Congruency is key.
- Be consistent. Doing so reinforces the achievement of those intentions; it is like building up a credit in the mind's bank of possibility.
- Belief becomes natural when you are behaving in a manner consistent with the success you seek.
- Find your inspiration (your why) rather than relying totally on external motivations to enjoy a fuller experience of what you engage in.
- To embrace your new experiences of success, something of your old ways of being must be relinquished. You can't have change if nothing changes.
- Believe what you bring to life in your mind's eye as a set intention is possible.

Taran Hughes

Afterword

Thank you again for being here with this book, not because you bought it – there are many such messages being shared – but because you, like so many others at this time, are awakening to a life purpose deeper than many of us have imagined for the longest time. This material has been prepared for sales professionals, but the sales dimension to it is merely an outer wrap for the core message that I am, along with many others, choosing to bring to the awareness of others right now.

Having read this book you are faced with a choice. You may put it down, reflect on how interesting or useful it was and go back to doing what you did before. However if anything contained within these pages has resonated with you, you can step into a new paradigm of experience within your career and perhaps your life. Having pulled back the curtain of your subconscious behaviours you can decide to put into practice what we have explored together to bring about significant change in your work life and to those around you. Your practice of raised state, set intentions and empowered belief will be felt by others and may well trigger their awakening to awareness.

Of course, there is a price to this. There cannot be growth without change; something of your old way of being will, by virtue of it no longer being of service to you, be let go of in order for you to embrace the richness that a life lived on purpose can offer you.

It is my belief our inner purpose is to awaken to the consciousness described in this book and our outer purpose is to bring that consciousness into everything we do.

~~~~~~~
~~~~~~~

Glossary

Egoic

In the context of this book, when speaking of ego and egoic behaviours it comes from the point of view that at the centre of pronouncements, ideas and thoughts a person may have the conceptual self of I, me, my or mine, which seeks to use the subject content, such that I, me, my or mine is being employed by the ego to enhance its sense of separateness from all other things. It does so in an attempt to enhance itself through inflation of the self or through making someone else smaller, wrong, bad etc.

Hawkins' scale of consciousness

The scale of consciousness, as discussed in the book *Power vs. Force* by Dr David Hawkins, is a hierarchical model of self-development using a scale spanning from 0 – 1000 which refers to the spectrum of human energetic states.

Left brain

Referring to thought sequenced in the linear style, which is commonly described as "logic" or "reason". Data is processed in a sequence A→B→C, analogous to a digital computer.

Limbic system

The limbic system comprises several brain structures associated with memory and emotion.

Paradigm

The dimensions of a context or field as limited by parameters that inherently predict one's perception of reality. A paradigm, generally, is a definition of one's perception of reality according to its limitations.

Presence
Presence points to the stillness of one's mind. It is that stillness of mind that anchors thoughtless awareness of what is happening in the present moment.

Qualification (in sales)
A core activity within sales practices, it is the process of evaluating the critical data components needed for a sale to be progressed and includes but is not limited to such basic details as who will make the decision to buy, and how the decision is arrived at. It includes the timeframe of the client need, if indeed there is one, together with any significant milestones on the client horizon that may adversely or positively influence the progression of the sales process and of course the allocated budget or whether monies can be made available to meet the cost of the solution or offering being discussed.

Sponsoring event
When speaking of a sponsoring event in the context of limiting beliefs we are referring to the root cause, the first occurrence of a negative event happening. From negative sponsoring events subconscious ideas form and these become limiting beliefs and ideas about oneself.

State
Refers to our inner condition or feeling of wellbeing at any given moment. It's well described as our sense of what is good and possible when in a high state and of hopelessness or apathy for things when coming from a very low energetic state, but in truth it is more than that. It is something we sense in others and we are susceptible to sudden changes in our own when things don't go the way we want.

About the Author

Taran Hughes is a successful sales professional now focusing on developing greater conscious awareness in the sales and business environments through his writing, talks and workshops.

Taran held leadership roles within the telecommunications industry for over 10 years, working with such organisations as SingTel, BT, AboveNet and Zayo. His passion and focus has always been to drive sales excellence and develop talent from within.

Taran delivers training and speaks on developing success-based mindsets and conscious awareness for sales professionals.

Made in the USA
Coppell, TX
12 May 2021